INTRODUCING

for Windows

CAROL MCKENZIE & PAT BRYDEN

Heinemann Educational Publishers,
Halley Court, Jordan Hill, Oxford OX2 8EJ
a division of Reed Educational & Professional Publishing Ltd

Heinemann is a registered trademark of Reed Educational
& Professional Publishing Limited

OXFORD BLANTYRE MELBOURNE AUCKLAND
IBADAN JOHANNESBURG GABORONE
PORTSMOUTH NH (USA) CHICAGO

First published 1998
01 00 99
10 9 8 7 6 5 4 3

A catalogue record for this book is available from the British Library on request.

ISBN 0 435 45426 9

Designed by Moondisks

Typeset by TechType, Abingdon, Oxon

Printed and bound in Great Britain by The Bath Press, Bath

Screen shots reprinted with permission from Microsoft Corporation

▶ Contents

▶ RSA Text Processing schemes

The Royal Society of Arts (RSA) Examinations Board has designed a suite of Text Processing schemes at Stages I, II and III. The overall aim of these modular awards is to meet the business document production requirements of the discerning employer and to give candidates the opportunity to demonstrate competence in text processing skills to the level demanded for NVQ Administration.

Stage I indicates that the candidate has sufficient knowledge or skill to begin employment, although further study would be beneficial.

Stage II shows a sound understanding of and competence in the subject and a recommendation for employment. It also suggests that someone who holds such a certificate may well benefit from advanced studies.

Stage III indicates an all-round knowledge and understanding of the subject and, in the practical skills, a very high degree of proficiency.

At each stage, there is a *Part 1* examination which assesses candidates' ability to produce a variety of routine business documents at that stage. A selection of *Part 2* examinations assesses skills in more specific applications such as word processing, typewriting, audio-transcription, word processing in foreign languages or using specialist vocabulary, etc.

Possession of Stage I Text Processing awards contributes significantly towards the evidence required for NVQ Administration Level 1 Elements 7.1 and 7.2.

▶ About this book

This book has been produced to assist people who wish to gain accreditation through the RSA Examination Board's Text Processing schemes, from pre-Stage I to Stage I, using Microsoft Word 97 for Windows software package. It is anticipated that users will be familiar with the QWERTY keyboard and have basic competence in using computer hardware.

This book covers the following assessment schemes.

▶ RSA CLAIT (Word Processing Application).

▶ RSA Initial Text Processing Skills.

▶ RSA Stage I Part 1 Text Processing.

▶ RSA Stage I Part 2 Word Processing.

Units 1–6 are designed for students preparing to take basic examinations such as RSA CLAIT (WP Application). These units are also suitable for beginners who wish to learn basic text processing skills without taking an examination.

Units 7–11 are designed for students preparing to take basic examinations such as RSA Initial Text Processing Skills. These units are also suitable for beginners who wish to learn basic text editing skills and the preparation of personal business letters without taking an examination.

Units 12–16 are designed for students preparing to take elementary examinations such as RSA Stage I Part 1 Text Processing. These units are also suitable for students who wish to extend their knowledge and skills to include preparation of memoranda and business letters without taking an examination.

Units 17–20 are designed for students preparing to take RSA Stage I Part 2 Word Processing. These units are also suitable for students who wish to extend their knowledge and skills to include simple tabulation and text formatting techniques without taking an examination.

A brief outline of the examination and examination practice for each stage of learning is included in Units 6, 11, 16 and 20.

Format of the book

Printout checks for all exercises are given at the back of the book (pp. 131–156). These should be used for checking by both students and teachers/trainers.

The Progress Review Checklist allows a record of progress through the exercises to be kept, noting the number of errors made. If completed at the end of each working session, this checklist can be referred to quickly in order to locate the unit to be worked next.

Command boxes for Word 97 functions are given when appropriate. Instruction is given on how to carry out the required function. The commands explain keyboard, mouse and menu operation.

The Glossary of Commands at the back of the book provides a comprehensive, alphabetically-listed quick reference for all the Word 97 commands introduced in the book. The commands are shown for keyboard, mouse and menu users. Shortcut keys are included and students may prefer to use these methods as they become more familiar with the program.

All exercise material is to be completed in Times New Roman point size 12 unless otherwise indicated.

Working through a unit

1   When you see this symbol, read all the information before you begin. You may also need to refer back to this information as you carry out the exercises.

2   When you see this symbol, carry out the exercises, following the numbered steps, e.g. **1.1**, **1.2**.

3   Use Word's spelling and grammar tool to check your document. Proofread the document carefully yourself – the spelling tool does not find every error.

4   Use the Print Preview facility to check that your document is going to be correct when printed. If it is, save your work on to your floppy disk (usually in A Drive) or into an appropriate directory. Then print your work.

5   Compare your document with the printout checks at the back of the book (pp. 131–156). (If you are using this book in class, your tutor may also wish to check your work.) Correct any errors which you find in your work. Print the documents again if required to do so by your tutor. (If you are working on your own, you may not consider this necessary.)

6   Complete your Progress Review Checklist. Then exit from Word 97 or begin work on the next unit (as appropriate).

Do not delete files from your disk – you may need them later!

▶ Introduction to Word 97 for Windows

Microsoft Windows is a graphical user interface, which allows the user to communicate with the computer. The graphical nature of the messages on screen makes Windows a user-friendly operating system. Microsoft Word 97 is a software package used for text processing which operates within the Windows environment.

The **mouse** is used to move a pointer to any required location on screen. The mouse has two buttons: *left* and *right*. As you move the mouse across the desk, an electronic sensor picks up the movement of the ball and moves the **mouse pointer** across the screen in the same direction.

▶ You use the mouse to *point* to the item you want on screen.

▶ You then *click* the mouse button (usually the left one) to highlight or *select* an option on screen (quickly pressing and releasing the button).

▶ Sometimes you *double-click* a mouse button (quickly pressing and releasing the button twice).

▶ You may also use a *dragging* action by holding down the mouse button, moving the mouse, and then releasing the button.

▶ If you are not sure of the function of an icon on one of the tool bars, just point to it with the mouse and wait for a second – a **tool tip** describing the function of the icon will appear to help you.

Figure 1 Tool tip

When you start the Word 97 program, the **Document Window** will be displayed on screen (Figure 2):

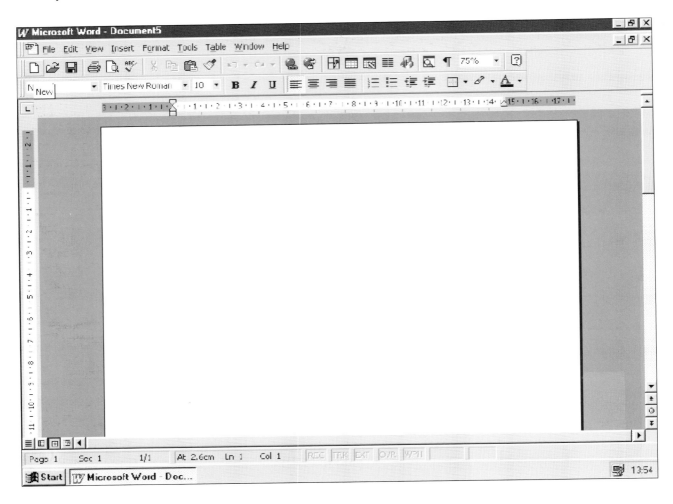

Figure 2 Document Window

The blue bar across the top of the screen is the **Title Bar**, showing the name of the application being used and the current document name.

The **Menu Bar** gives a list of **menu names** describing commands which can be selected by using the mouse or the keyboard.

Figure 3 Menu bar

A **drop-down menu** then gives a further range of options within the **menu** (in Figure 4, the <u>V</u>iew menu has been selected).

As you will see, some of the menu choices have one character underlined (e.g. **<u>R</u>uler**). Selection can be carried out using the keyboard, eg pressing **R** in the example in Figure 4 would remove the Ruler line from the screen. The Ruler returns if you press **R** again – this is a 'toggle' switch. (A tick against a menu choice indicates that the option is currently in operation. When the tick is removed, the facility is 'switched off'.)

Selection can also be made by using the mouse. Clicking the left mouse button on **<u>R</u>uler** the example in Figure 4 would remove the Ruler line from the screen.

Some menu choices are followed by a **keyboard shortcut**, eg

<u>F</u>ind...	**Ctrl + F**
Re<u>p</u>lace...	**Ctrl + H**
<u>G</u>o To...	**Ctrl + G**

Figure 4   Drop-down menu

Holding down the **Ctrl** key and then pressing the letter shown will activate the command.

An **ellipsis** (three dots ...) after a menu choice (eg **<u>Z</u>oom...**) indicates that you will be asked to give more information before the command can be executed.

When Word needs to give or receive more information, a **dialogue box** is displayed on screen. You can move through the dialogue box using the Tab key or you can move the mouse pointer to the box required and click the left button. Word asks you to respond by presenting information, options or questions in different ways by using boxes and buttons. The dialogue box in Figure 6 shows the different types of boxes and buttons you will meet.

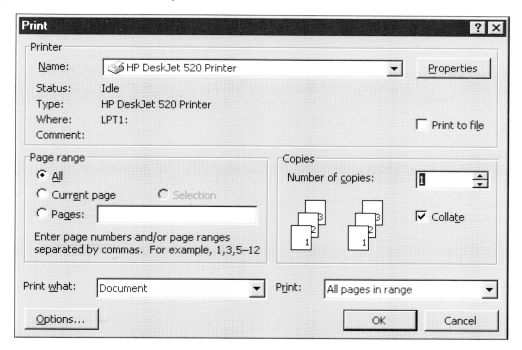

Figure 5   Dialogue box

Clicking on [OK] confirms the information in the boxes. You can close a dialogue box without giving a command by clicking on [Cancel] or on the [X] close icon at the top right of the dialogue box.

You can minimise a document window by clicking on the [_] **Minimise** icon. This reduces the window to a small bar at the bottom of the window.

To restore the window to its full size, click on the [⊡] **Restore window** icon.

When Word is carrying out a function, it may ask you to wait. The icon for this is the [⧗] hourglass. Wait until the hourglass has disappeared from the screen before proceeding with the next step.

The **Standard Tool Bar** is displayed on screen whilst you are working on a Word document.

Figure 6   Standard Tool Bar

This consists of a range of **icons**, each representing a different function related to creating and editing documents. You select a function by pointing to the icon with the mouse pointer and clicking the left mouse button. For example, clicking on the [🖨] **Print** icon would activate the printer to print a copy of the current document.
The use of these icons is explained more fully throughout the book.

The **Formatting Tool Bar** is also displayed on screen in a Word 97 document.

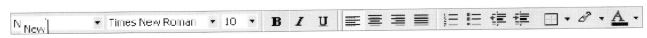

Figure 7   Formatting Tool Bar

This consists of a range of icons, each representing a different formatting option. You select a function by clicking on the icon. The use of these icons is explained more fully in Units 3, 5, 17 and 18.

The function activated by each icon is shown in a **Tool Tip**, which appears when the mouse pointer is positioned on the icon (see the **Spelling and Grammar** icon tool tip on page 5).

When an icon button is shown as having been *pressed in*, (appears in a lighter colour [**B**]), this indicates that the function is currently in operation, i.e. any text keyed in would be formatted in bold.

The **Status Bar** at the bottom of the screen displays information about the document on screen for example, the page number, section number, line number, column number, etc.

Figure 8   Status Bar

The current time is displayed in the bottom right-hand corner of the screen.

The **Scroll Bars** at the right side and bottom of the screen allow text to be scrolled by the use of the mouse.

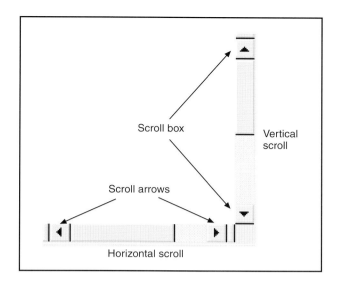

Figure 9 Scroll bars

For example, clicking on the  down vertical scroll arrow button will move the 'document frame' downwards so that the text moves up the screen. Scrolling is more fully explained in Unit 1.

The horizontal Scroll Bar also displays buttons to select the different ways in which a document can be viewed. These are more fully explained in Unit 3.

Figure 10 Scroll bar buttons

The **Task Bar** at the very bottom of the screen allows you to switch between applications or tasks.

Figure 11 Task Bar

Word offers users two forms of online help. The **Help** command can be activated in three ways from the document screen.

1 By selecting **Help** from the Menu Bar and then clicking on the [?] **Microsoft Word Help** icon.
2 By clicking on the **Microsoft Word Help** icon on the Standard Tool Bar.
3 By pressing the **F1** function key on the keyboard.

Activating **Help** in any of the above ways brings an animated character (your **Office Assistant**) on to your screen, followed by a yellow text box asking 'What would you like to do?'

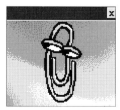

Figure 12 Office Assistant

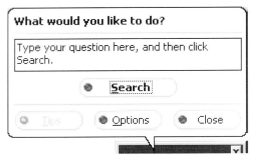

You can type in a question in your own words and then click Search. Office Assistant will then show you a list of topics related to your question or to the task in hand. Clicking on the appropriate blue button will give you the information you need.

Figure 13 What would you do?

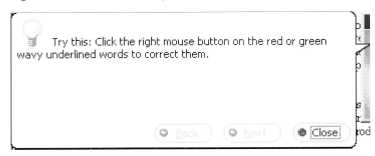

You may also click **Tips** to see screen tips.

Note: Office Assistant can change its appearance – from 'The Genius', ' Power Pup', 'Shakespeare' and 'The Dot' to name but a few! If you would rather not see these delightful characters on your screen, you can 'switch them off' by:

Figure 14 Tip

▶ clicking on the **Close** button on the Assistant's box
▶ clicking the right button anywhere in the Assistant's box and selecting **Hide Assistant**
▶ clicking the right button anywhere in the Assistant's box and selecting **Options** then clearing the **Respond to F1** box.

Clicking the ✎ **Contents and Index** icon on the **Help** drop-down menu allows you to:

▶ open a **book** containing information on Word functions (**Contents**); or
▶ key in the topic on which you need help (**Index**).

Figure 15 Help Menu

Clicking the ▶? **What's This?** icon on the **Help** drop-down menu changes the mouse pointer into a question mark so that you can click on a particular item and learn about it.

unit 1

▶ Learning the basics

By the end of Unit 1 you should have learnt how to:

- ▶ load Word 97 for Windows
- ▶ open a new document
- ▶ key in text
- ▶ move around the text using the mouse, arrow keys and Scroll Bar
- ▶ edit text – delete/insert characters or words
- ▶ split and join paragraphs
- ▶ proofread your work carefully
- ▶ save your document to your personal disk or to a directory
- ▶ print your document
- ▶ clear the screen by closing a file
- ▶ exit from Word 97 for Windows

Exercise 1A ▶

Follow the instructions step by step.

1.1   Load Windows and select Word 97 for Windows by double-clicking on the 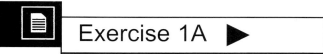 icon *or* by selecting Programs and then  from the Start menu.

The application (document) window (Microsoft Word) will be displayed on screen. Refer to page 00 of the Introduction to refresh your memory on this.

1.2   Open a new document using one of the methods described below.

Open a new document ▶

Keyboard	Mouse
Press: **Ctrl + N**	Select: **File** from the Menu Bar
	Select: **New** from the File drop-down menu
	OR
	Click: The ☐ **New (New file)** button on the Standard Tool Bar

The **New** dialogue box is displayed on screen

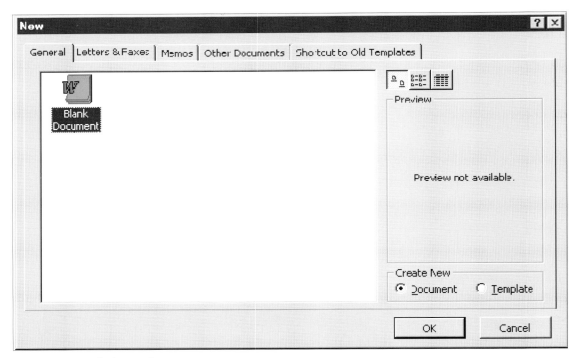

Figure 1.1   New dialogue box

Check that your dialogue box matches the one shown in Figure 1.1.

▶   Check: That the **Document** button is selected under **Create New**.

▶   Click: **OK**

▶   *Or* double-click: The **Blank Document** icon.

Key in text
Word wrap
When you key in text, you do not need to press ↵ (return/enter) when you want to start a new line as Word will do this for you automatically.

Initial capitals
To type an initial capital (first letter of a word):

Press: **Shift** key and the letter

Note: It is good practice to operate the Shift key with the other hand when you want to type one capital letter. For example, to key in a capital J, hold down the left Shift key with the left little finger and type the J with the right index finger.

Closed capitals
(All letters in capitals):

Press: **Caps Lock** key (to start typing in capitals)
Press: **Caps Lock** again to stop

Clear lines

To leave a blank line, eg between paragraphs:

Press: ⏎ twice

Note: You should leave at least one clear line after headings. You should also leave one clear line space between paragraphs and different parts of a document.

Punctuation

Full stop
No space before; one or two spaces after – be consistent.

Comma
No space before, one space after.

Question/exclamation mark
Same as full stop because they are used at end of sentence.

Colon (:)
No space before. Two spaces after when followed by a capital letter. One space after when followed by a lower-case letter

Semi-colon (;)
No space before, one space after.

Brackets and single/double quotation marks
One space before the opening sign. One space after the closing sign. No spaces immediately inside the signs.

 Exercise 1A (continued) ▶

1.3 *Note:* All exercises should be keyed in using the Times New Roman font in point size 12. If you are not sure how to set up Word to do this, consult your tutor or refer to page 45 in Unit 5.

Refer to the information section above: (Key in text). Key in the following text – do not worry if you make mistakes; you can correct them later.

A word processor allows text to be created and printed quickly and accurately. Text can be stored on disk or in a directory for future use. You can recall text and modify or rearrange it if you want to make changes without having to type it out again. The ability to edit text in this way should save paper as printing can be done only when the document is perfect. Two advantages of word processing have been increased productivity and more efficient use of resources. Improvements in printer technology have enabled high-quality text to be produced at great speeds.

1.4 As you keyed in the above text, you should have noticed a vertical black line | at the point where you were inserting text. This is the insertion pointer and it moves along as you key in text. The arrow keys (←↑→↓) to the right of the main keyboard allow you to move the insertion pointer | around the text one space or one line at a time.

Practise moving the insertion pointer around the text you have just keyed in using the arrow keys.

1.5 The insertion pointer can also be moved around the text by using the mouse. If you move the mouse on your desk, you will see the I beam moving correspondingly on screen. If the left-hand mouse button is clicked, the I beam changes into the insertion pointer.

Practise positioning the insertion pointer in the text you have just keyed in, using the mouse and the I-beam.

1.6 *Check the text you have keyed in very carefully.* If you find any errors, correct them now by positioning the insertion pointer at the appropriate place and deleting or inserting characters or words as required, using the commands shown below.

 ## Delete/insert text

Keyboard/mouse

To delete (erase) an incorrect character:

Position the insertion pointer: Immediately *after* the character to be deleted.
Press: ← **Delete (Del)** (the backspace delete key).

OR

Position the insertion pointer: Immediately *before* the character to be deleted.
Press: ← **Delete (Del)**.

To insert a character (or characters):

Position the insertion pointer: Where the text is to be inserted.
Key in: The text (the existing text will move across to make space for the new text).

Note: If you find that text is being typed over previous text, press the key marked **Ins (**or **Insert)** to correct this.

 1.7 Position the pointer immediately after the full stop at the end of the text on screen. Press ↵ (return/enter) twice to start a new paragraph. Key in the following text under your previous work.

> Word Processors are often used for general commercial correspondence such as letters and memos. However, the advantages of the technology are perhaps demonstrated to best effect in the production of reports. Such documents are often long and need to be revised several times.

Functions such as headers, automatic page numbering and spelling checks are of great assistance to the operator. Many commercial workers can prepare their own reports without having to use the services of an operator.

Mailmerge allows letters to be combined with a database of names and addresses to produce documents, which appear to be personal to the recipient. Companies can send out a mail shot to prospective customers using this facility.

1.8 You have already practised moving around the text using the arrow keys and the mouse pointer. In Word 97 you can move around the text more quickly using the keyboard keys. If you learn and practise these commands, you will become more proficient. Some of these commands are particularly useful in a long document.

Practise moving the insertion pointer around the text you have just keyed in using the keyboard commands shown below.

 ## Moving around the text: quick methods

To move	Keyboard
Left word by word	Press: **Ctrl** + ← (arrow key) (hold down the Ctrl key and press the ← key whilst the Ctrl key is still held down)
Right word by word	Press: **Ctrl** + →
To the end of the line	Press: **End**
To the start of the line	Press: **Home**
To the top of a paragraph	Press: **Ctrl** + ↑
To the bottom of a paragraph	Press: **Ctrl** + ↓
Up one screen	Press: **Page up**
Down one screen	Press: **Page down**
To the top of the document	Press: **Ctrl + Home**
To the bottom of the document	Press: **Ctrl + End**

 1.9 Check the text you have keyed in very carefully, comparing it with the exercises. If you find any errors, correct them now by moving the insertion pointer to the appropriate position and deleting or inserting characters or words as required.

1.10 Follow the instructions 'Save and name a document' to save your document on Drive A or in an appropriate directory on your PC or network, using the filename **EX1A**.

Note: If you are saving your work on to disk, you will use Drive A, inserting the disk into the disk drive of your computer. If you are saving your work on to the hard disk or a network file server, you need to use the appropriate drive and directory names: check with your tutor or a technician if you are not sure.

Save and name a document ▶

Keyboard	**Mouse**
Press: **Ctrl + S** or **F12** (function key at top of keyboard)	Select: **File** from the Menu Bar Select: **Save As**... from the **File** drop-down menu

The Save As dialogue box is displayed on screen (Figure 1.2).

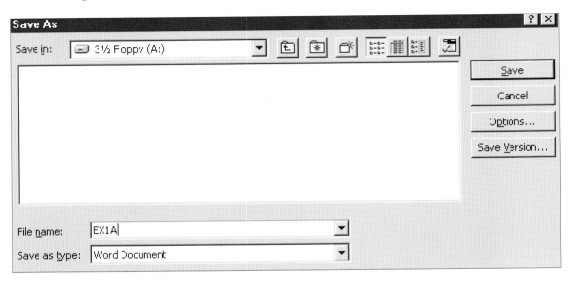

Figure 1.2 Save As dialogue box

Select from the Save As dialogue buttons as follows:

▶ Click: In the **File name** box and key in **EX1A**
▶ Click: ▼ at side of the **Save in** box and select $3\frac{1}{2}$" **Floppy (A:)** (or appropriate drive)
▶ Check: That the **Save as type** box shows **Word Document**
▶ Click: the **Save** button

Note: You can move between the different sections of a dialogue box by using the Tab key or by positioning and clicking the left mouse button.

'Word is saving EX1A.DOC' should appear in the status line at the bottom of the screen. These words may come and go so quickly that you do not notice them!

If the hourglass icon appears on the screen, wait until it has disappeared – long documents can take some time to save. The document should remain on your screen.

1.11 The first draft of a document is often edited. The writer may decide to delete or insert words or to make other changes. You have already learned how to delete and insert text. Now read about splitting and joining paragraphs.

Splitting paragraphs/joining paragraphs

As part of editing a document, it may be necessary to split a block of text into two or more smaller paragraphs. It may also be necessary to join two or more paragraphs to make a larger paragraph.

To split a block of text into two paragraphs:

▶ Position the insertion pointer: Immediately before the first letter of the intended second paragraph
▶ Press ↵ return/enter twice

To join two paragraphs into one:

▶ Position the insertion pointer: Immediately before the first letter of the second paragraph
▶ Press: ← **Del** (delete/backspace) twice

 # Exercise 1A (continued)

Practise editing the text you saved as EX1A by referring to the instructions given. Make the following changes to the document on screen as shown below:

▶ delete any words crossed out
▶ insert text at points marked Λ
▶ make new paragraphs at all the points marked // or W₀
▶ join the paragraphs at the run-on sign (⌐——⌐)
▶ in the third paragraph, change the word **commercial** to **office**.

> A word processor allows text to be created and printed quickly and accurately. Text can be stored on disk or in a directory for future use. You can recall text and modify or rearrange it if you want to make changes without having to type it out again. The ability to edit text ~~in this way~~ should save paper as printing can be done only when the document is perfect. [Two advantages of word processing have been increased productivity and more efficient use of resources. Improvements in printer technology have enabled high-quality text to be/produced at great speeds. (attractively)
>
> Word Processors are often used for general commercial correspondence such as letters and memos. However, the advantages of the technology are perhaps demonstrated to best effect in the production of reports. Such documents are often long and need to be revised several times.⌐
>
> ⌐Functions such as headers, automatic page numbering and spelling checks are of great assistance to the operator. Many commercial workers can/prepare their own reports (now) without having to use the services of an operator. Λ
>
> Mailmerge allows letters to be combined with ~~a database of~~ names and addresses to produce documents, which appear to be personal to the recipient. Companies can send out a mail shot to prospective customers using this facility.

1.12 Check your work on screen, comparing it with the exercise. When you are satisfied that your document is completely accurate, follow the instructions under 'Save a document (previously named)' to save the changes you have made.

 ## Save a document (previously named)

You should use this method when you have amended a document and want to save it under the same name.

The document on screen was saved under the filename **EX1A** before you carried out the changes. The amended document can now be resaved using the same filename.

Keyboard	Mouse
Press: **Ctrl + S**	Select: **File** from the Menu Bar Select: **Save** from the **File** drop-down menu
OR	OR
Press: **Shift + F12**	Click: The **Save** button on the Standard Tool Bar

'Word is preparing to background save EX1A.DOC' should appear in the status line at the bottom of the screen. These words may come and go so quickly that you do not notice them!

If the hourglass icon appears on screen, wait until it has disappeared – long documents can take some time to save. The document should remain on your screen.

 1.13 You have already practised moving around the text using the arrow keys, the mouse pointer and the keyboard quick methods. In Word, the text can be moved up and down the screen (scrolling). In scrolling, the insertion pointer stays in the same position but the text moves up or down.

Refer to page 9 of the Introduction to refresh your memory on scroll bars and scroll buttons, and practise using the scroll bars, watching the effects on your document on screen.

 ## Scrolling the text (using the mouse) ▶

To scroll the text	Mouse
One line at a time	Click: Up and down scroll arrows ▲ ▼
One screen at a time	Click: In the grey Scroll Bar immediately underneath or above the appropriate scroll arrow
Quickly over larger distances	Click and drag: The thumb box (small unmarked grey button) on the vertical Scroll Bar (a text box appears to tell you where you are within the document – which page) OR Click: Anywhere in the Scroll Bar

1.14 Your first document (EX1A) should now be amended and saved. To print a copy of the document, follow the instructions under 'Print a document'.

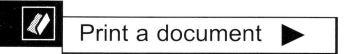

Print a document ▶

Keyboard

Press: **Ctrl** + **P**

Mouse

Select: **File** from the Menu Bar

Select: **Print** from the **File** drop-down menu

The Print dialogue box is displayed on screen (Figure 1.3).

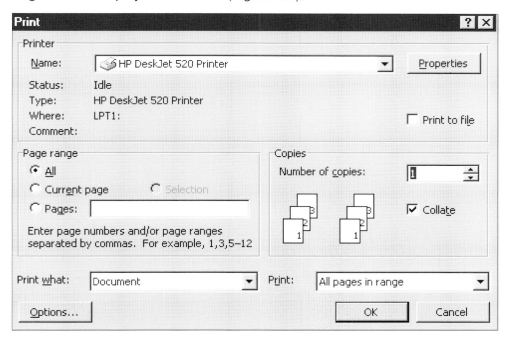

Figure 1.3   Print dialogue box

Printer: the Name of the printer should be displayed.

Page Range: allows selection of pages printed – normally displays **All**.

Copies: allows choice of number of copies printed – normally displays **1**.

Print what: allows choice of what is to be printed – normally displays **Document**.

Print: allows certain pages to be printed – normally displays **All Pages in Range**.

Click: **OK**

'Word is preparing to background print EX1A.DOC' should appear in the status line at the bottom of the screen. Wait until the hourglass icon has disappeared from the screen – long documents can take some time to print. The document should remain on your screen.

 1.15 Check your printout with the key. If you find any errors, correct them on screen, save your document again and print again if necessary.

1.16 Follow the instructions under 'Close a file' to clear your application window.

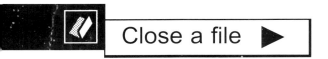

Close a file ▶

After saving and printing in Word for Windows, the document remains on screen. Close the file before opening another one, or before exiting the program.

Keyboard	Mouse/menu
Press: **Ctrl + W**	Select: **File** from the Menu Bar
	Select: **Close** from the **File** drop down menu

If you have *not* saved your file, the dialogue box shown in Figure 1.4 will be displayed on screen.

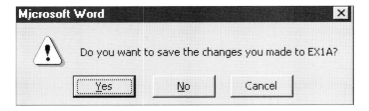

Figure 1.4 *Save changes?*

▶ Click: **Yes** to save the latest amendments to your document (this is usually what you want to do).

▶ Clic: **No** ONLY if you are sure that you do not want to save the amendments you made after last saving the document.

▶ Click: **Cancel** at any time if you are not sure – you will return to the document.

If you saved your file immediately before closing it, you will return to the Microsoft Word application window.

 1.17 Exit the program if you have finished working or continue straight on to the next unit.

Exit from Word 97 for Windows ▶

After closing all your document files, the Microsoft Word application window is displayed on screen.

Keyboard	Mouse/menu
Press: **Alt + F4**	Select: **File** from the Menu Bar
	Select: **Exit** from the **File** drop-down menu

OR double-click: The **Close** button at the top right of the application window

unit

2

▶ Manipulating text

By the end of Unit 2, you should have learnt how to:
- ▶ open an existing file
- ▶ select text
- ▶ delete a block of text
- ▶ restore deleted text
- ▶ move a block of text
- ▶ copy a block of text
- ▶ insert a block of text (paragraph)

Open an existing file ▶

Keyboard	Mouse
Press: **Ctrl + O**	Select: **File** from the Menu Bar Select: **Open**
	OR
	Click: The **Open** button on the Standard Tool Bar

The Open dialogue box is displayed on screen (Figure 2.1).

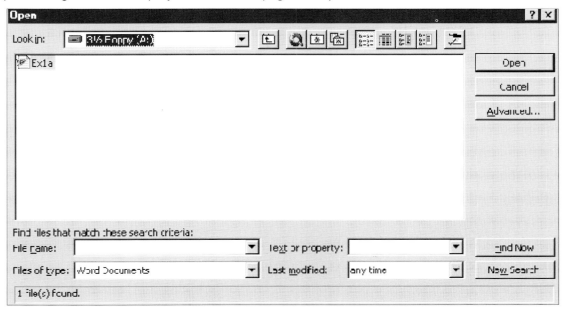

Figure 2.1   Open dialogue box

► Check that the **Look in** box shows $3\frac{1}{2}$" **Floppy (A:)** (or appropriate directory).

► The **Files of type** box should show **Word Documents**.

► A list of the files on your disk should be displayed.

► Move the pointer to the file you require and click the left button – the filename will be highlighted in blue.

► Double-click: The filename *or* Click **Open** (The file will appear on screen).

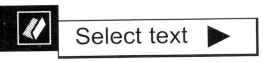

Select text ►

When you want to change a block of text in some way, it is necessary first of all to shade or highlight the particular section of text. In Word, this is called 'selecting' text. The selected text shows in reverse – white letters on a black background, eg **selected text**

To select:	Keyboard	Mouse
One character (or more)	Press: **Shift + →** or Press: **Shift + ←** (*repeat until all required text is selected*)	Click and drag: The mouse pointer across the text
One word	Position the mouse pointer: At the beginning of the word; Press: **Shift + Ctrl + →**; *or* Press: **Shift + Ctrl + ←**	Double-click: On the word
To the end of the line	Press: **Shift + End**	Click and drag: The mouse pointer right or down
To the beginning of the line	Press: **Shift + Home**	Click and drag: The mouse pointer left or up
A full line	Position the pointer: At the beginning of the line; Press: **Shift + End** *OR* Position the pointer: At the end of the line: Press: **Shift + Home**	Click: In the left margin (the selection border) next to the required line
A paragraph		Double-click: In the selection border *OR* Triple-click: Within the paragraph
The whole document	Press: **Ctrl + A**	Triple-click: In the selection border
Any block of text		Position the pointer: At the beginning of the text; Hold down: **Shift**; Click: At the end of the text

Delete a block of text

To delete larger portions of text you *select* the block of text you wish to delete and then operate the commands for deletion.

Select: The text to be deleted (*See Select text, above*)

▶ Press: **Del(ete)**; *or*
▶ Press: ← (backspace/delete key)

 ## Quick delete and insert text

To delete an incorrect section of text (of any size) and replace with correct text (of any size), simply select the incorrect text and key in the new text.

Select: The text to be deleted (*see Select text, above*)

Without moving the insertion point;
Key in: The new text (*The incorrect text which was initially selected will disappear*)

 ## Restore deleted text (undo)

You can restore text that has been deleted accidentally provided that you do so straightaway. It is important that the pointer is in the correct place before you begin.

Keyboard	Mouse
Press: **Ctrl + Z**	Select: **Edit** from the Menu Bar Select: **Undo Typing**
	OR
	Click: The 🔄 **Undo** button on the Standard Tool Bar.

Word allows you to 'undo' many previous actions. These can be accessed by clicking on the 🔽 button to the right of the **Undo** button. You may like to try using this facility later in your learning programme – it may be a little confusing at this stage.

Move a block of text

You can move sections of text quickly without deleting and retyping. This facility is sometimes called 'cut and paste'. Text to be moved is 'cut' and placed on the 'clipboard', and then 'pasted' into its new position.

Keyboard	Mouse
Select: the block of text to be moved	
Press: **F2** Move the pointer to: The new position Press: ↵	Select: **Edit** from the Menu Bar Select: **Cut** (the text disappears from the screen and is put on the clipboard) Move the pointer to: The new position Select: **Edit** from the Menu Bar Select: **Paste** (the text reappears in its new position)
OR	*OR*
Press: **Ctrl + X** (the text disappears from the screen) Move the pointer to: The new position Press: **Ctrl + V** (the text reappears in its new position)	Click: The ✂ **Cut** button on the Standard Tool Bar Move the pointer to: The new position Click: The 📋 **Paste** button on the Standard Tool Bar
	OR
	Move the pointer to: The new position. Hold down: **Ctrl** and click the **right mouse button**

 ## Copy a block of text

Copying a block of text means that the text will remain in its original place in the document and a copy of the same text will also appear elsewhere. This facility is sometimes called 'copy and paste' – a copy of the text to be 'copied' is placed on the 'clipboard' and then 'pasted' into its new position.

Select: The block of text to be copied.

Keyboard	Mouse
Press: **Ctrl + C** Move the pointer to: The required position Press: **Ctrl + V**	Select: **Edit** from the Menu Bar Select: **Copy** (the text remains on screen and a copy is put on the clipboard) Move the pointer to: The required position Select: **Edit** from the Menu Bar Select: **Paste** (a copy of the text appears in its required position)

OR

Click: The 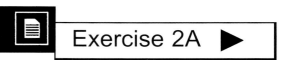 **Copy** button on the Standard Tool Bar

Move the pointer to: The new position

Click: The **Paste** button on the Standard Tool Bar

Exercise 2A ▶

2.1 Open the file you saved in Unit 1 (filename EX1A).

2.2 Practise selecting, deleting, restoring, moving and copying blocks of text on the document on screen (EX1A) until you feel confident about the functions.

After this practice, your document may not be exactly as you saved it! Close the file without saving the changes – Word will ask you if you want to save the changes you made to 'EX1A.doc?' Select: **No**.

Exercise 2B ▶

2.3 Open EX1A again. Add your name and a heading to the top of the document as follows:

▶ Position the pointer at the top left of your document (the status line at the bottom of the screen should show Ln 1 Col 1).

▶ Press: ↵ twice to make two clear lines.

▶ Press: ↑ twice to reposition the pointer at the top of the document.

▶ Key in: Your full name.

▶ Press: ↵ twice to leave a clear line.

▶ Key in: The heading **INTRODUCTION TO WORD PROCESSING**.

(There should be one clear line between your name and the heading and one clear line between the heading and the text.)

2.4 Amend the document as instructed below:

▶ *Delete* paragraph A (follow instructions for selecting and deleting a paragraph).

▶ *Restore* paragraph A (follow instructions for restoring text).

▶ *Delete* the circled words in paragraph B (follow instructions for selecting and deleting words).

▶ *Move* paragraph C so that it appears under paragraph A (follow instructions for selecting and moving a block of text).

▶ *Copy* the heading **INTRODUCTION TO WORD PROCESSING** to E (follow instructions for selecting and copying a block of text).

Your name

INTRODUCTION TO WORD PROCESSING

(A) A word processor allows text to be created and printed quickly and accurately. Text can be stored on disk or in a directory for future use. You can recall text and modify or rearrange it if you want to make changes without having to type it out again. The ability to edit text should save paper as printing can be done only when the document is perfect.

(B) Two advantages of word processing have been increased productivity and (more) efficient use of resources. Improvements in (printer) technology have enabled high quality text to be (attractively) produced at great speeds.

(C) Word Processors are often used for general office correspondence such as letters and memos. However, the advantages of the technology are perhaps demonstrated to best effect in the production of reports. Such documents are often long and need to be revised several times. Functions such as headers, automatic page numbering and spelling checks are of great assistance to the operator. Many office workers can now prepare their own reports without having to use the services of an operator.

(D) Mailmerge allows letters to be combined with names and addresses to produce documents which appear to be personal to the recipient. Companies can send out a mailshot to prospective customers using this facility.

(E) *

2.5 You are now going to insert a new paragraph into the document.

▶ Position the pointer: At the beginning of the second paragraph – the one beginning 'Word Processors are often …' .

▶ Press: ↵ twice (to insert two blank lines).

▶ Press: ↑ twice.

▶ Key in: The following paragraph:

In the past, typists spent a considerable amount of time in re-typing documents that needed to be amended. Sometimes, a large part of a document had to be re-typed because deleting or adding text altered the page numbering and layout.

2.6 Make sure there is one clear blank line above and below the paragraph you have just inserted.

2.7 Compare your work on screen with the printout check. If you find any errors, correct them now.

2.8 Save your file, using the new filename EX2B. (Refer to the instructions in Unit 1 – 'Save and Name a Document'.)

2.9 Print a copy of your work.

2.10 Exit the program if you have finished working, or continue straight on to the next unit.

unit 3

► Changing margins and line spacing

By the end of Unit 3, you should have learnt how to:

► change the document format in the following ways:

- – ragged right margin
- – justified right margin
- – inset left margin
- – inset right margin
- – double-line spacing

► change the unit of measurement
► preview a document before printing

 ## Formatting the right margin ►

Look at this paragraph – particularly at the ends of the lines. The left margin is straight, but the right margin is 'ragged' (the lines do not end at the same point). This paragraph is formatted with a *ragged* (or unjustified) right margin.

In Word, you can adjust the text so that the right margin is also quite straight as shown in this paragraph. This is called a *justified* right margin (all the lines – except the last – end at exactly the same point).

It is normal practice to use either a justified right margin or a ragged right margin for a document – but not a mixture of the two formats. The left margin is always justified so a request to use a justified margin means fully justified, ie on both sides. Word may be set 'by default' to a ragged or a justified right margin. You can change the default settings if required. The margin format you are currently using is displayed on screen by the alignment buttons on the Formatting Tool Bar. The alignment style currently in use will be shown as a depressed button and in a lighter shade.

The choices of text alignment are as follows:

Align Left   Center   Align Right   Justify

Experiment by pointing to the alignment icons in turn and waiting for a few seconds for the Tool Tip giving the above labels to appear.

Note: when setting margin alignment for continuous text, you will use only **Align Left** ('ragged right' or 'unjustified' margin) and **Justify** (both margins justified, sometimes called 'fully justified').

You may set the right margin format you require before you key in a document. Alternatively, you may change the format during or after keying in.

When you are working on the exercises in this book and during RSA examinations, you may choose whether to use a ragged or justified right margin *unless you are otherwise instructed*.

Ragged (unjustified) right margin

To set the format for a document before keying in:

Keyboard	Menu Bar	Standard Tool Bar
Press: **Ctrl + L**	Select: **Format** from the Menu Bar Select: **Paragraph** Select: **Left** from the **Alignment** drop down menu Click: **OK**	Click: The [≡] **Align Left** button on the Standard Tool Bar

To set the format for a document after keying in:

Keyboard/mouse

Select: The document or the paragraph (see instructions in Unit 2) and then operate one of the methods shown above.

Justified right margin

To set the format for a document before keying in:

Keyboard	Menu Bar	Standard Tool Bar
Press: **Ctrl + J**	Select: **Format** from the Menu Bar Select: **Paragraph** Select: **Justified** from the **Alignment** drop down menu Click: **OK**	Click: The [≡] **Justify** button on the Standard Tool Bar

To set the format for a document after keying in:

Keyboard/mouse

Select: The document or the paragraph (see instructions in Unit 2) and then operate one of the methods shown above.

Changing left and right margin widths ▶

In Word 97, you can change the format of a document by increasing or decreasing the size of the margins. You can use this facility to change the margins for the whole of a document or for certain sections only.

> Insetting the margins is often used to draw the reader's attention to a particular piece of information – like this!

The left and right margins are usually preset at 3.17 cm or $1\frac{1}{4}$ in. When you open a new document and request a Blank Document, the preset (default) margins automatically come into use. Even if the text appears to fill the document window, the default margins will be used on the page when it is printed. The documents you have already printed should demonstrate this to you.

You may be given instructions to use margins in inches or in centimetres (or in both). The default setting in Microsoft Word is centimetres. If you wish, you could change the **Units of Measurement** to inches and make these the default. The unit you choose (inches or centimetres) would then be used throughout the program in all relevant dialogue boxes.

Note: When you are working on the exercises in this book, retain the default setting of centimetres unless otherwise instructed by your tutor. RSA examinations give measurements in centimetres, although past papers may also show inches.

Change the units of measurement
To change to centimetres:

▶ Select: **Tools** from the Menu Bar
▶ Select: **Options**
▶ Click: The **General** tab to bring this 'card' to the front
▶ Open: The **Measurement** units drop-down menu by clicking on the ▼
▶ Click: **Centimetres**
▶ Click: **OK**

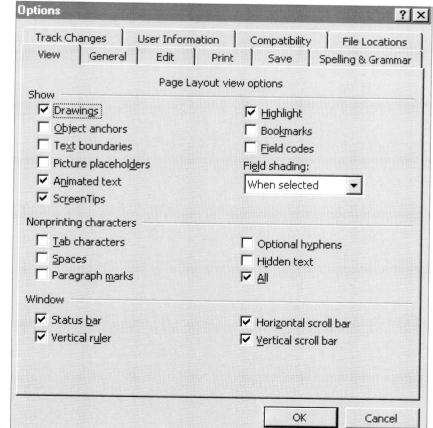

Figure 3.1 Options dialogue box

To change to inches:

Follow instructions as above, selecting **Inches** in the **Measurement Units** drop-down menu.

Margins

To set left and right margins before keying in:

Mouse/Menu Bar

Specify **Page Setup**:
Select: **File**
Select: **Page Setup**
Click: The **Margins** tab to bring this 'card' to the front

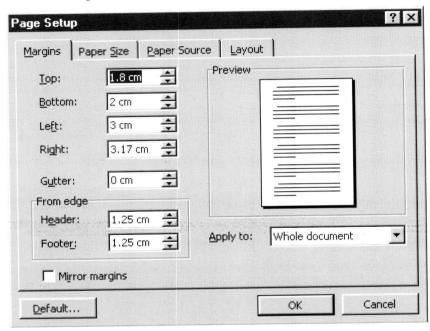

Figure 3.2 Page setup dialogue box

Click: The **Left** spin box (or move there by pressing the **Tab** key)
Key in: The required measurement (or use the arrows to increase or decrease the measurement displayed

Click: The **Right** spin box and repeat the above
Open: The **Apply to** drop-down menu by clicking on the
Click: **Whole document**
Click: **OK** to operate changed margins for this document only
(You can click on **Default** to adopt these margins as the settings for all future new documents.)

Mouse/ruler markers

Check: That you are in **Page Layout View**

Click: The ▣ **Page Layout View** icon at the bottom left of the screen

Display the ruler on document screen:

Select: **View** from the Menu Bar
Select: **Ruler** unless it is already selected with a ✔ (the ruler is displayed at the top of the document screen) (Figure 3.3)

Figure 3.3 Ruler

To change the left margin:

1   Move the pointer to the left margin boundary on the horizontal ruler (where dark grey and white sections of the ruler meet); the **Left Margin** tool tip appears.

2   When the pointer changes to a ↔ double-headed arrow, press and hold down the Alt key and the left mouse button; the current margin and typing line measurements are displayed on the ruler line between arrows (Figure 3.4).

3   Move the pointer to left or right to drag the margin boundary to the required measurement.

4   Release the Alt key and the mouse button.

To change the right margin:

▶   Move the pointer to the right margin boundary on the ruler (where dark grey and white sections of the ruler meet); the **Right Margin** tool tip appears.

▶   Repeat margin setting method as steps 2–4 above.

Using this method, the horizontal ruler will display the left and right margin measurements, and the typing line length measurements all at the same time (Figure 3.4).

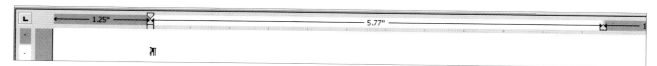

Figure 3.4 Horizontal ruler

To reset margins for a document after keying in:

Keyboard/mouse

Select: The document (**Ctrl + A**) and then operate either of the methods shown above.

To reset margins for a document after keying in:

Keyboard/mouse

Select: The text (see instructions in Unit 2) and then operate either of the methods shown above.

Line spacing: single and double

In Word 97, you can format the text to appear in double-line spacing (i.e. one blank line between each line of text).

This paragraph is formatted to double-line spacing, which is another method of

emphasis and is used to highlight a particular portion of text. Draft documents

are often produced in this spacing so that amendments can be easily marked.

Sometimes, in double-line spacing, it is very difficult to tell where one paragraph

ends and another starts if the last line of the first paragraph is a long one. For

example, can you tell that there is a new paragraph at the beginning of the 4th

line of text – the one beginning 'Sometimes, in double line spacing …' ?

A paragraph in double-line spacing format looks better if it has an extra line

space above and below it (as in the example shown here). This 'separates'

the paragraph from others in single-line spacing.

When working in double-line spacing, if you press the ↵ Return/Enter key twice at the end of a sentence as usual, there will be *three* clear lines between each paragraph. When you are changing line spacing for sections of a document during editing, you may find that line spacing between paragraphs becomes inconsistent. In an examination, consistency of presentation is important and you should always check through your document and correct any inconsistencies in line spacing before printing.

One extra line space can be added or removed by using **Ctrl + 0** (zero). Pressing the keys once adds a line space; pressing the keys again deletes a line space. This method can be used to give *two* clear lines between paragraphs. Sometimes, the three clear lines produced by the formatting method can make a document containing many paragraphs rather long. You can use **Ctrl + 0** to adjust the line spacing above and below paragraphs, by one extra line only, to improve the appearance and legibility of your document.

Sometimes, only certain portions of a document are presented in double-line spacing and this gives particular emphasis to that part of the text. Word displays double-line spacing on screen if this format has been selected but the default setting is single-line spacing.

Note: When you are working on the exercises in this book and during RSA examinations, you will be requested to use only single and/or double-line spacing – no other options are required.

Line spacing: single and double

To set line spacing before keying in:

Keyboard	Mouse/Menu Bar
Press: **Ctrl + 2** for double-line spacing Press: **Ctrl + 1** for single-line spacing Press: **Ctrl + 0** to add a line space Press: **Ctrl + 0** again to remove a line space	Select: **Format** from the Menu Bar Select: **Paragraph** Click: The **Indents and Spacings** tab to bring this 'card' to the front Open: The **Line spacing** drop-down menu by clicking on the ▼ button Click: **Double** or **Single** (as required)

To change line spacing in an existing document:

Keyboard/Mouse/Menu Bar

Select: The text (as previously described) and then operate the commands shown above.

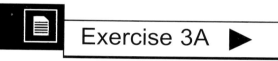

Exercise 3A ▶

3.1 Open the file you saved at the end of Unit 2 if it is not already on your screen. The filename is **EX2B**.

3.2 Practise using the justification facility within the document on screen. Change the whole document to display a *justified* right margin. Then change back again to a *ragged* right margin. Next, practise changing the margin justification for a single paragraph, eg make the first paragraph *justified* and the rest of the paragraphs *ragged*.

3.3 Change the unit of measurement currently being used to *centimetres* if it is not already in this mode.

3.4 Practise changing the margins within the document on screen. Increase both the margins for the whole document by 2 cm. Next, decrease the right margin only by 1 cm.

3.5 Practise changing the line spacing within the document on screen. Change the whole document from single to double-line spacing. Then change the first paragraph back to single-line spacing. Try a few more changes of this type. Practise using **Ctrl + 0** to add or remove extra line spaces between paragraphs. Remember that you are aiming for consistency in spaces between paragraphs.

3.6 After this practice your document may not be exactly as you saved it! Don't worry – close the file without saving the changes.

3.6 Reopen the file **EX2B** before beginning the next exercise.

Print Preview ▶

When you have made changes to the format of a document, it is useful to preview before you print. You can then check that the correct changes have been made and you can see the layout of the document as it will be when printed.

Print Preview

Keyboard	Mouse
Press: **Ctrl + F2** (A toggle switch which changes between Print Preview and Normal View)	Select: **File** from the Menu Bar Select: **Print Preview** *OR* Click: The 🔍 **Print Preview** button on the Standard Tool Bar

The Print Preview screen is displayed on screen (Figure 3.5).

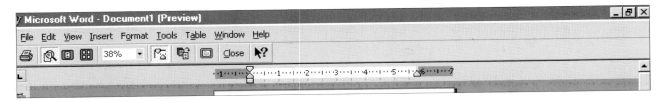

Figure 3.5 Print preview screen

The Print Preview Tool Bar is displayed at the top of the window. The current page is shown in reduced size

Select from the following options to view and check your document:

Type of View	Keyboard	Mouse
Normal View (*the default view*)	Press: **Ctrl + F2** (toggles between Normal View and Print Preview)	Select: **View, Normal** from the Menu Bar *OR* Click: ▤ **Normal View** on the horizontal scroll bar (first button on left)
Page Layout View (*as will be printed*)	—	Select: **View, Page Layout** from the Menu Bar *OR* Click: ▤ **Page Layout** on the horizontal scroll bar (third button from left)
Print Preview (*shows pages in reduced size*)	Press: **Ctrl + F2** (toggles between Normal View and Print Preview)	Select: **File, Print Preview** from the Menu Bar *OR* Click: The 🔍 **Print Preview** button on the Standard Tool Bar *Note*: Click: The ▣ **One Page** button or the ▦ **Multiple Pages** button on the **Print Preview** screen to view the required number of pages

Zoom (*magnifies part of document*)	—	Click: ▼ at the right of the ⎯18%▼⎯ **percentage** box on the **Print Preview** screen and select a figure OR Click: The 🔍 **Magnifier** button on the **Print Preview** screen and then click on the document
Full View (*menus and buttons not displayed*)	—	Click: The ▣ **Full Screen** button on the **Print Preview** screen

Shrink to Fit

If your document has only a small amount of text on the last page, you can use the 🔲 **Shrink to Fit** icon within Print Preview to reduce the length of your document by one page. Take care that the font size does not become too small to read though!

Editing in Print Preview

It is possible to use the Menu Bar for some editing functions whilst in Print Preview, e.g. you may change margins using the 📐 **View Ruler** icon and line spacing and justification in the usual ways, although it is probably easier to do this editing in normal or page layout view.

Printing from Print Preview

It is possible to print your document from the Print Preview screen by pressing the 🖨 **Print** icon – the whole of the current document will be printed. However, it is not generally recommended to use this method of printing because you have no control over the number of copies or the selection of pages to be printed. The same icon is displayed on the Standard Tool Bar – its use is not recommended for the same reasons.

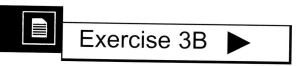

Exercise 3B ▶

3.7 Reformat the document as follows – refer to the instructions for changing the format of the margins and the line spacing:

▶ use a ragged (unjustified) right margin;
▶ set both left and right margins at 2.5 cm or 1 in; and
▶ change the format of the second paragraph only to double-line spacing.

3.8 Practise using the Print Preview screen and buttons to view and check your document, comparing it with the printout for EX3B.

If your layout is correct, proceed to the next step. If your layout is not correct, reread the instructions for formatting to get the layout right. You can edit your work within the Print Preview screen or you can return to Normal View to do this.

3.9 Save your file using the filename **EX3B**.

3.10 Print a copy of your work.

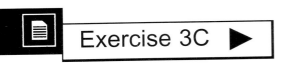

Exercise 3C ▶

3.11 Reformat the document you have just printed as follows:

▶ use the fully-justified format (left and right margins justified);

▶ inset left and right margins by a further 1.27 cm or $\frac{1}{2}$ in (add 2.5 cm + 1.27 cm = 3.77 cm); and

▶ use double-line spacing for the fourth paragraph only.

3.12 Print Preview your document comparing it with the printout for EX3C.

If your layout is correct, proceed to the next step. If your layout is not correct, reread the instructions for formatting to get the layout right. You can edit your work within the Print Preview screen or you can return to Normal View to do this.

3.13 Save your file using the filename **EX3C**.

3.14 Print a copy of your work.

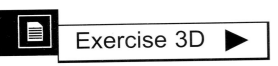

Exercise 3D ▶

In exercises 3A, 3B and 3C, you learned how to reformat a document by changing the line spacing and margins after keying in. In Exercise 3D, you will practise changing the line-spacing and margins as you key in the text.

3.15 Turn back to Page 32 and key in the text on that page, starting with the heading **Line Spacing: single and double** and ending at the end of the first paragraph of the section in single line spacing – '... inconsistencies in line spacing before printing'.

Refer to the instructions 'To set left and right margins before keying in' to inset the left and right margins after the first paragraph. Add 2 cm to both margins, i.e. change from 3.17 cm to 5.17 cm.

Refer to the instructions 'To set line spacing before keying in' at the same point in the text – to change the line spacing setting before keying in the paragraphs in double-line spacing.

Don't forget to leave extra line spaces between paragraphs in double line-spacing. (The instructions are in the text on Page 32).

Reset the left and right margins to default settings (3.17 cm) before typing the paragraph in single line-spacing – 'When working in double...'.

3.16 Print Preview your document comparing it with the printout for EX3D at the back of the book. If your layout is not correct, re-read the instructions for formatting to get the layout right. You can edit your work within the Print Preview screen or you can return to normal view to do this.

3.17 Save your file using the filename **EX3D**.

3.18 Print a copy of your work.

3.19 Exit the program if you have finished working or continue straight on to the next unit.

unit 4

▶ Checking spelling and grammar, finding and replacing text

By the end of Unit 4 you should have learnt how to:

▶ use AutoCorrect and AutoFormat

▶ check spelling and grammar in a whole document or in a block of text

▶ find (search) and replace text in a document

 ## Automatic correction of common keying-in errors

You will probably have noticed that as you type, Word will automatically correct some commonly misspelt words. For example, if you type 'teh' instead of 'the' or 'adn' instead of 'and' or 'i' instead of 'I', Word will put it right for you – try it! If there is a word that you often mistype or misspell, you can add it to Word's list of automatic corrections.

AutoCorrect (Figure 4.1)

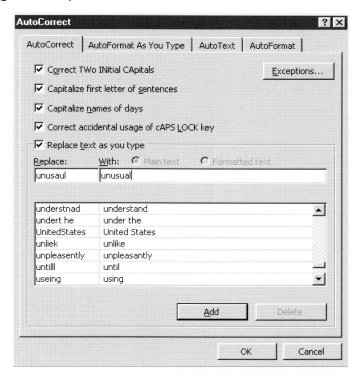

Figure 4.1 AutoCorrect

▶ Select: **Tools**, **AutoCorrect** from the menu
▶ Check: That the **Replace Text As You Type** check box is ticked
▶ In the **Replace** box, key in: The word you often mistype/misspell, e.g. unusaul
▶ Key in: The correct spelling of the word in the **With** box, e.g. unusual
▶ Click: **Add**, **OK**

Word will also make the following corrections automatically:

▶ Change the second capital letter to a lower-case letter if you accidentally type two capital letters at the beginning of a word.
▶ Capitalise the first letter at the beginning of a sentence.
▶ Capitalise the first letter of the days of the week.
▶ Reverse accidental usage of the cAPS LOCK key.

AutoFormat

Whilst you are typing a document, Word's AutoFormat automatically applies certain formats to items such as headings, numbers, symbols, etc. You can decide which formatting changes you want Word to make, or you can turn off AutoFormat completely. When you first start Word, AutoFormat is turned on by default. With **AutoFormat** selected, some examples of Word's automatic formatting include the following:

▶ If you type a number followed by a full stop, hyphen, bracket or greater than sign (>), and then a space or tab and text, Word makes the text a numbered list. (Press: **Enter** twice to end the list.)
▶ If you type an asterisk, hyphen, or greater-than sign (>), and then a space or tab and text, Word makes the text a 'bulleted' list, ie inserts the symbol at the beginning of all lines.
▶ If you type three or more dashes, underscores, equal signs, asterisks, tildes (~) or number signs (#) above a paragraph, Word places a horizontal border above the paragraph: a thin line for hyphens, thick line for underscores, double line for equal signs, single wavy line for tildes, decorative line for number signs.
▶ A fraction, such as 1/2 or 1/4, is converted to $\frac{1}{2}$ or $\frac{1}{4}$.
▶ An ordinal number, such as 1st, is converted to 1st.
▶ Straight quotation marks (' and "), are converted to smart (curly) quotes ('....') and ("......")
▶ Elements in a letter, eg the salutation Dear Mr Jones, prompt the Letter Wizard.

To turn AutoFormat on:

Select: **Format**, **AutoFormat**, from the menu
Select: **AutoFormat now** button

To turn on specific AutoFormat features:

Repeat the above
Click: The **Options** tab
Click: The **AutoFormat** tab
Check: That the options you want on are ticked
Click: **OK**

To turn AutoFormat off:

Select: **Format**, **AutoFormat**, from the menu
Click: The **AutoFormat** tab
Clear: The options you do not want (ie click on the option to remove the tick)
Click: **OK**

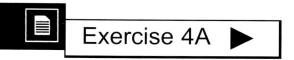

Exercise 4A ▶

4.1   Start a new file. Retaining the errors shown, note what Word does as you key in the text:

THe 1st day of teh week is monday. i will order an extra 1/2 pint of milk.

As you key in, Word should automatically correct the sentence to:

The 1ˢᵗ day of the week is Monday. I will order an extra $\frac{1}{2}$ pint of milk.

If not, follow the instructions to turn on AutoCorrect and AutoFormat and repeat step 4.1 again.

4.2   Clear your screen without saving the file.

 # Spelling and grammar check ▶

Word has a built-in spelling and grammar check facility which checks as you type for spelling and grammar errors. The Spellcheck memory contains thousands of words, but doesn't include many proper names (eg cities, surnames, etc). If you were going to use an unusual word fairly frequently that is not already in the Spellcheck memory, you have an option to *add* it to the list. Spellcheck would never stop on that word again, unless you had keyed it in wrongly of course!

As you key in the text, Word will identify a spelling error with a red wavy line and a grammatical error with a green wavy line. Automatic spell and grammar checking is very useful but you must also proofread the text yourself. The Spellcheck facility simply compares each word you have keyed in with its own 'dictionary' of words. If you have keyed in the wrong version of a word, eg *their* instead of *there,* spellcheck will not detect this as both versions are spelt correctly. Only you can tell if you have copied names of people or places correctly and if a piece of information you were asked to find is correct. You can choose to act only on those words you want to change – if Word queries a word which you know to be correct, you can ignore Word's prompt to change it.

Another useful feature of Word's grammar check is that it will also find two spaces left accidentally between words, except after a full stop.

Spelling and grammar check: quick method

Click: The right mouse button on a word with a wavy line
Click: The right move button on the correction you
want from the list offered

Figure 4.2   Spelling and grammar check: quick method

Spelling and grammar tool: to turn on/off ▶

You can choose to check spelling and grammar automatically as you type. However, if you find the wavy lines distracting, you can turn the facility off temporarily and then check the entire document all at once after typing.

Select: **Tools**, **Options** from menu
Click: The **Spelling and Grammar** tab

To turn the facilities *on*

Click: **Check spelling as you type**
        Check grammar as you type

To turn the facilities *off*

Click: **Hide spelling errors in this document**
        Hide grammatical errors in this document

Spelling and grammar check: dialogue box method

Keyboard	**Mouse**
Position the cursor at the start of the file	Position the cursor at the start of the file
Press: **F7**	Select: **Tools**, **Spelling and Grammar** from the menu
	OR
	Click: The **Spelling and Grammar** button

The Spelling and Grammar dialogue box is displayed on screen (Figure 4.4).

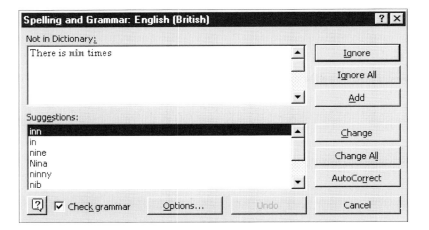

Figure 4.4 Spelling and Grammar dialogue box

▶ Word tells you the error in the dialogue box and tells you what type of error it is.
▶ Word highlights the most obvious replacement in the **Suggestions** box and often gives a list of other likely alternatives for you to select.
▶ You can also edit the text yourself in the dialogue box if this is more appropriate.

Select from the spelling dialogue buttons as appropriate:

Button	Action
Ignore	Leaves the word unchanged the first time it occurs but stops on it whenever it occurs again (if you continue editing, the word **Ignore** changes to **Resume**).
Ignore All	Leaves the word unchanged on every occurrence (until you restart Word).
Change	Accepts the spelling in the dialogue box or the **Suggestions** box.
Change All	Changes the first and all subsequent occurrences of the misspelt word.
Add	Adds the word to the Dictionary.
AutoCorrect	Adds the misspelt word and its correction to the AutoCorrect list – i.e., if you ever misspell this word in the same way again as you are typing, Word will correct it automatically for you!

Press: **Esc** to finish   Select: **Cancel** to finish

Note: If you do not wish to check the spelling of the whole document, you can first select/highlight a portion of text or even one word before running Spellcheck.

  Exercise 4B ▶

4.3   Start a new file. Key in the following text – retain all the deliberate spelling and keying-in mistakes (these have been circled) for the purpose of this exercise.

Hellebores of the Family Ranunculaceae

This popular english garden plant brightens the collorless months of winter. Delicate cup-shaped flowers, in shades of dark purple to dusky pink and primrose yellow to white, hang from folliage which often doubles as a superb evergreen soilcover.

Some types of hellebores will thrive in the most awkwaard dry shadey places, but they cannot stand being waterlogged. It is possible to propagate hellebores by division around september but many types of hellebores are very generous self-seeders. Each seedling will differ slightly from its parent and could provide a distinct new vareity.

Professional breaders continually search for significant differences that can be developed to create new flowers. All parts of the plant are poisonious and even the sap is irritant so it is advisable to wear gloves for protection when handling. Some speicies of hellebores can cause facial deformities in the ofspring of animals that eat the plant.

4.4   Move the cursor to the top of the document and run the spelling and grammar check facility.

The word **Ranunculaceae** will be queried – this is because the word is not in the Spellcheck dictionary although it is not necessarily spelt incorrectly. Check that you have copied the word correctly. If so, select **Ignore**.

The word **english** will be queried – this is because the word should have an initial capital. Make the change.

4.5 Continue to check the document, either accepting or replacing text as appropriate.

4.6 Save and print your document using filename **EX4B**. Check your printout with the key. If you find any errors, correct them on screen, save your document again and print again if necessary.

 # Find (search) and replace

In word processing, it is possible to find a given word or phrase automatically and exchange it for another given word throughout a document. An example of the way in which this function could be used is a letter being sent out from school to parents. It would be very easy to produce some letters that referred to 'your son' and some that referred to 'your daughter', or every occurrence of 'he' could be changed to 'she'.

You can use Word's find and replace function in two different ways (the first method is the safer in examinations):

1 You can ask Word to stop every time it has located the 'find' word and wait for your confirmation before it 'replaces' the word (**Replace**). If you find an entry that you do not wish to be changed, you can skip over it and move to the next occurrence of the search (**Find Next**).

2 You can allow Word to go straight through the document 'finding and replacing' without stopping for confirmation from you (**Replace All**).

Find (search) and replace text

Keyboard	**Mouse and Menu**
Press: **Ctrl + H**	Select: **Edit, Replace**

The Replace dialogue box is displayed on screen (Figure 4.3).

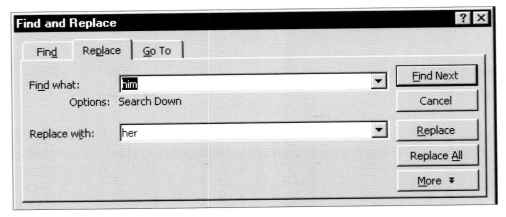

Figure 4.3 Replace dialogue box

- ► In the **Find what** box, key in: The text to be searched for
- ► In the **Replace with** box, key in: The replacement text
- ► Click: The **Find next** button

Select from the find and replace dialogue buttons as appropriate:

Button	Action
Find Next	Skips an entry which you do not wish to be changed and moves to the next occurrence of the search.
Replace	Allows control over each replacement one at a time.
Replace All	Replaces all occurrences automatically.
More	Displays more advanced find and replace criteria. **More** changes to **Less** when you decide to select more advanced criteria. This option includes the following:
Match Case	to find the exact combination of upper- and lower-case letters.
Find whole words only	to find occurrences that are not part of a larger word, (eg the word 'rate' could appear in i*rate*, c*rate*, desec*rate*d).
Format	to replace text formatting, e.g. replace bold with underline.
Special	to find special characters such as paragraph mark, graphic, etc.
Search	**All** – search through all the document. **Down** – search from the insertion pointer to the end of the document. **Up** – search from the insertion pointer to the start of the document.
Press: **Esc** to finish	Select: **Cancel** to finish

Find text (without replacing)

If you only want to *find* text (without replacing it) similar commands can be accessed through the **Find** dialogue box – Select: **Edit**, **Find** from the Menu *or* Press: **Ctrl + F**.

Tip: Sometimes you can't see the text under the dialogue box so you can't decide whether to replace or not! Using the mouse, point to the middle of the horizontal blue bar running across the top of the dialogue box and drag the box down to the bottom left or right of the screen.

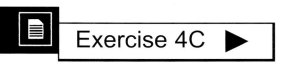 Exercise 4C ►

4.7 Retrieve the file **EX4B** from your disk (unless it is already on your screen) and, using the search and replace function,

- ► change **types** to **varieties** (two occurrences in the second paragraph);
- ► change **breeders** to **growers** (in the third paragraph); and
- ► change **flowers** to **blooms** (in the first and third paragraphs).

4.8 Change the format of the document as follows:

- ► justified right margin;
- ► double-line spacing for first paragraph only; and
- ► inset both margins by 1.27 cm ($\frac{1}{2}$ in).

4.9 Preview the file to check the format changes. Save and print your document using filename **EX4C**. Check your printout with the key. If you find any errors, correct them on screen, save your document again and print again if necessary.

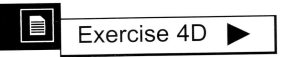

Exercise 4D ▶

4.10 Retrieve the file **EX2B** from your disk. Using the search and replace function,

▶ change **produce** to **generate** (in the fourth and fifth paragraphs – note in the fourth paragraph that Word finds *produce* as part of *produced*);

▶ change **often** to **frequently** (two occurrences in the third paragraph); and

▶ change **INTRODUCTION TO** to **BENEFITS OF** in the title and at the end of the document.

4.11 Change the format of the document as follows:

▶ justified right margin;

▶ double-line spacing for second paragraph; and

▶ inset left margin only by 1.27 cm $\frac{1}{2}$ in).

4.12 Preview the file to check the format changes. Save and print your document using the filename **EX4D**. Check your printout with the key. If you find any errors, correct them on screen, save your document again and print again if necessary.

unit 5

▶ Improving text presentation

By the end of Unit 5, you should have learnt how to:

▶ emphasise text, before typing and during editing, using bold, italics, underline and highlight (shading)

▶ use alignment of text centred across the page as a means of text emphasis

▶ change the appearance of text by changing the font typeface and point size

Formatting/emphasising text ▶

You have already practised using CAPITALS, inset margins and double-line spacing as methods of text emphasis. In Word 97, formatted/emphasised text is displayed on screen as it will appear when printed on paper. Some additional methods of formatting or emphasising text are as follows:

BOLD Bold type (heavy print to make it look darker) is a method of emphasising words or phrases (especially headings) to make them more noticeable and to stress their importance to the reader.

UNDERLINE Underline is used in a similar way to embolden to add emphasis to text.

ITALIC Italic can also be used to emphasise text – it is more commonly used within the main body of the document.

FONT TYPEFACE Another way of emphasising the text would be to change the font typeface, e.g. *This is typed in Brush Script.* **Wide Latin,** *Mistral.*

FONT POINT SIZE The default point size of text for word processed documents is usually 10 or 12 points. The actual size of the printed text, however, is relevant to the typeface being used – even if you select the same point size for different fonts they will not always appear as the same size. For example,

a) This is typed in 10 point ■ Braggadocio typeface

b) This is also typed in 10 point – Kino MT typeface

HIGHLIGHT Highlighting text using different colours and shades will make it **stand out** . It is a useful feature for emphasising headings, etc.

CENTRED TEXT	Centring of text, particularly main headings, emphasises the text. Main headings are often centred while subheadings are typed at the left margin. The centring function is useful when preparing certain documents such as menus or notices, where an attractive display is important.

You could choose a larger point size for subheadings or main headings in a document, or even a different font. It is not considered good practice to use too many different fonts – usually two will be sufficient otherwise the document can appear fussy and amateurish, although several point sizes of the same font typeface are acceptable.

You may be asked to remove text formatting/emphasis, eg changing text from bold to normal type, removing underline, etc.

How to format/emphasise text

Format/emphasis	Keyboard	Mouse
Bold	Press: **Ctrl + B**	Click: The **B** **Bold** button
Italics	Press: **Ctrl + I**	Click: The *I* *Italics* button
Underline	Press: **Ctrl + U**	Click: The **U** Underline button
Highlight text		Click: The 🖊 **Highlight** button
		Click: On ▼ to select a colour from the drop-down palette
Centre text	Press: **Ctrl + E**	Click: The ≣ **Centre** button
Change font	Press: **Ctrl + Shift + F**	Click: The Arial **Font** button
	Click: On ▼ and select a font from the list	Click: On ▼ and select a font from the list
Change font size	Press: **Ctrl + Shift + P**	Click: The 10 ▼ **Font Size** button
	Then press the ↓ or ↑ arrow to increase or decrease	Click: On ▼ and select a point size from the list
Next larger point size	Press: **Ctrl + Shift + >**	
Next smaller point size	Press: **Ctrl + Shift + <**	
Remove text emphasis/ back to plain text	Select: Text to change back	Select: Text to change back
	Press: **Ctrl + Space Bar**	Reselect: 'Standard' point size or font
Change lower case to all capitals	Select: Text to capitalise	Select: Text to capitalise
	Press: **Ctrl + Shift + A**	Select: **Change Case** from the **Format** menu, then **Uppercase**

To format text while typing:

▶ Click: The appropriate command button (eg click on the **B** button to switch bold text on); *or*
▶ Press the appropriate keys (eg press **Ctrl + B** to switch bold text on).
▶ Key in: The text.
▶ Click: The appropriate command button again to switch off the emphasis; *or*
▶ Press the appropriate keys again to switch off the emphasis.

To format existing text:

►   Select the text to be changed.
►   Click: The appropriate command button; *or*
►   Press the appropriate keys.

To remove emphasis from text:

►   Select: the emphasised text.
►   Click: The appropriate command button or press the appropriate keys to deselect the feature.

Exercise 5A ►

5.1   Start a new file:

Click: The **B** **Bold** button on the Formatting Tool Bar
Type: **This sentence is typed in bold**.
Click: The **Bold** button again to stop bold
Press: ↵

Click: The **U** **Underline** button on the Formatting Tool Bar
Type: <u>This sentence is typed with underline.</u>
Click: The **U**(nderline) button again to stop underline.
Press: ↵

Click: The ▤ **Centre** button on the Formatting Tool Bar
Type: This sentence is centred.
Press: ↵ (text should now be centred on screen)
Click: The **Left-align** button to return text to the left margin

Type: This sentence is typed with highlight.
Click: The ✎ **Highlight** button on the Formatting Tool Bar and drag the pen icon across the sentence
you just typed. It should now appear as: This sentence is typed with highlight.
Click: The ✎ **Highlight** button again to stop highlight
Press: ↵

5.2   Choose a different font style from the selection shown in the Font box on the Formatting Tool Bar and apply this to the first sentence.

5.3   Choose a different point size from the selection shown in the Font Size box on the Formatting Tool Bar and apply this to the last sentence.

5.4   Practise applying and removing the different methods of text emphasis for a few minutes. Delete the text on your screen – you do not need to save or print your work.

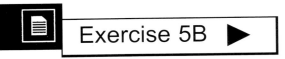
5.5   Starting a new file, key in the following short programme. Use the font Times New Roman, point size 12. Centre the text.

Draft copy

Mayton Vale Choir

Autumn Programme

Fit As A Fiddle
You Are My Lucky Star
All I Do Is Dream Of You
(Singin' In The Rain)

I Got Rhythm
Someone To Watch Over Me
Nice Work If You Can Get It
(Crazy For You)

Any Dream Will Do
Close Every Door To Me
One More Angel
(Joseph And The Amazing Technicolor Dreamcoat)

MAYTON VILLAGE HALL
WEDNESDAY 20 OCTOBER 1998, 7.30 PM
ALL SEATS £2.50

5.6   Save your document using filename **EX5B**. You do not need to print out your work yet.

5.7   Reformat the text following the instructions and the amendments to the layout shown below. You will need to refer back to the instructions 'Formatting/emphasising Text' given earlier in the unit.

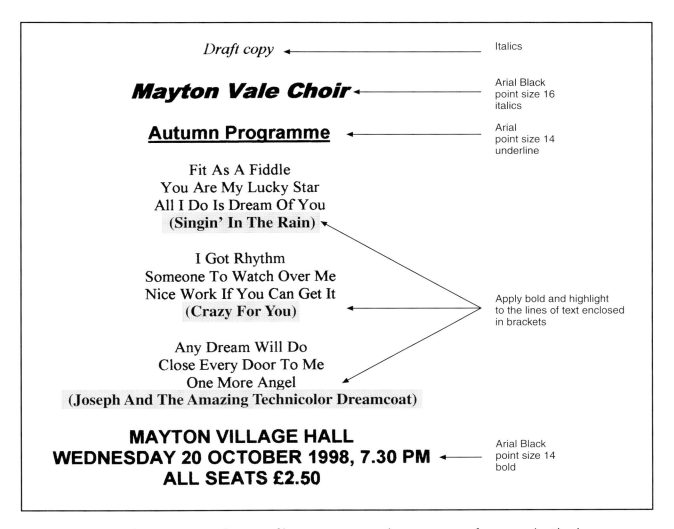

5.8 Save your document using the same filename **EX5B** and print a copy of your work. Check your printout with the example above and correct any errors if necessary.

5.9 You are now going to use text emphasis to create a standard file for a business memorandum head. You will recall this memo template later in Unit 13 when you will learn more about business memos – the purpose of this exercise is to practise using text emphasis for effective display.

Starting a new file, key in the following text, centring both lines and using the text emphasis indicated:

5.10 Save and print your document using filename **Memohead**. Check your printout with the key. If you find any errors, correct them on screen, save your document again and print again if necessary.

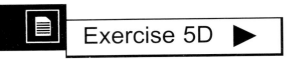

5.11 You are now going to use text emphasis to create a standard file for a business letterhead. You will recall this file later in Unit 14 when you will learn more about business letters – the purpose of this exercise is to practise using text emphasis for effective display.

Starting a new file, key in the following text, using right justification and the text emphasis indicated:

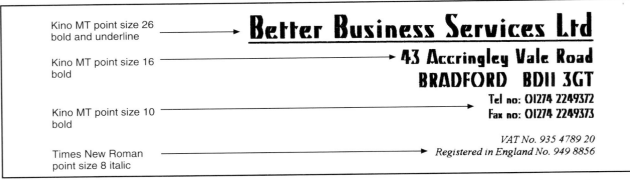

5.12 Save and print your document using filename **Letterhead**. Check your printout with the key. If you find any errors, correct them on screen, save your document again and print again if necessary.

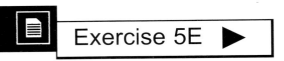

5.13 Clear your screen. Retrieve the file you saved as EX5B and make the following amendments:

▶ On the first line, remove italics from the words **Draft copy** and replace with bold. Change the justification from centred to left justified for this line only.

▶ On the second line (**Mayton Vale Choir**), remove italics and replace with highlight.

▶ Change the Arial font typeface to Mistral and increase by one point size (ie, in the headings **Mayton Vale Choir** and **Autumn Programme**, and also in the last three lines).

▶ Change the headings **Mayton Vale Choir** and **Autumn Programme** to all capitals.

▶ Remove the bold and highlight from the bracketed text and replace with italics.

5.14 Save and print your document using filename **EX5E**. Check your printout with the key. If you find any errors, correct them on screen, save your document again and print again if necessary.

5.15 Exit the program if you have finished working or continue straight on to the next unit.

unit 6

▶ Examination Practice 1

By the end of Unit 6, you should have completed a mock examination for the RSA CLAIT (Computer Literacy and Information Technology) Word Processing application.

✔ RSA CLAIT (Computer Literacy and Information Technology) Stage I Word Processing Application ▶

The CLAIT scheme provides a system of assessment through the completion of practical tasks. Word Processing is just one of 14 applications in the scheme.

If you are preparing to be assessed under the above scheme, Unit 6 will help you with the word processing application but you need to refer to other learning materials for additional applications such as spreadsheets, databases, etc.

If you are preparing for text processing awards rather than CLAIT, you should complete the exercises in Unit 6 as consolidation practice.

Assessments may be carried out in a registered centre under the supervision of a local assessor when both you and your assessor feel that you are ready. Your work will be marked by the local assessor and then checked by RSA's Marking Co-ordinator.

Examination hints

When completing your assessment:

- ▶ you may use your own notes or a manual prepared by the centre or the software manufacturer;
- ▶ put your name, centre number and printout number on each sheet;
- ▶ work through the tasks in the order in which they are printed;
- ▶ check your work very carefully before printing;
- ▶ hand in your printouts in the correct order;
- ▶ you may have a second fresh attempt at the same assignment if the first is not satisfactory;

You are now ready to try a mock assessment for CLAIT word processing. Take care and good luck!

The performance criteria for this assessment are detailed. To be sure that you have reached the required standard to be considered ready for the assessment, you need to work through several past papers and have these 'marked' by a tutor or assessor who is qualified and experienced in this field.

Results

If your finished work has no more than three data entry errors (eg wrong word, missing word, extra word) and if you follow the instructions carefully and completely, you will pass the assignment.

Successful completion of three applications merits a Stage I pass. A Profile Certificate is awarded if the performance criteria are not completely fulfilled.

Results are confirmed to the centre where you take the assessment.

Exercise 6A ▶

6.1 Load your program and, starting a new file, key in the following text using a left-aligned format (i.e., ragged right margin). Don't forget to type your full name at the top of the document.

COMMUNICATIONS

It may be 'good to talk' but is it always cheap? If you are using a hotel phone to communicate the answer could be different from what you think. In America, many hotels will charge visitors for calls even if they are unable to get through! Hotel phone charges vary, but one survey revealed that many hotels add between 400% and 800% more than a home based call.

Many visitors have been so alarmed by huge bills they have vowed not to return to hotels which charge such astronomical rates.

Following the barrage of angry complaints, some hotels are now relaxing their rules as they realise that the profit made on charges is being negated through loss of repeat custom.

Some hotels are reversing the trend and charging for the cost of the call only, but many previously bitten visitors now take one of the national phone charge cards with them as a precaution.

Another major cause of concern has been the practice of some hotels in making a charge for freephone numbers.

6.2 Use the Spellcheck facility to check your work for spelling errors. Compare your work *on screen* with the printed text above. Proofread carefully and make any necessary amendments.

6.3 Save and print your document using filename **EX6A**. Check your printout with the printed exercise above. If you find any errors, make the necessary corrections.

Exercise 6B ▶

6.4 Retrieve **EX6A** if it is not already on your screen.

6.5 Delete the paragraph beginning **Many visitors ...**

6.6 In the paragraph beginning **Another major cause ...** insert the word **customer** before concern, and insert the words **what are usually** before **freephone**.

6.7 Insert the following paragraph after the first paragraph:

Customers have complained that it would be cheaper to use their mobile telephones than to use the hotel's telephone facilities.

6.8 In the paragraph beginning **Following the barrage ...**, insert the words **inflated telephone** after the words **profit made on**.

6.9 In the first line of the first paragraph change **are using** to **dial out from**. Replace the word **phone** with **telephone** throughout the document.

6.10 Reformat the document to

▶ first paragraph only in double-line spacing;
▶ justified right margin; and
▶ both margins insetted by 1.27 cm ($\frac{1}{2}$ in).

6.11 Centre, embolden and underline the heading.

6.12 Move the last paragraph which begins **Another major ...** so that it becomes the fourth paragraph.

6.13 Replace the word **visitors** with **customers** wherever it occurs (twice in all).

6.14 Save and print your document using filename **EX6B**. Check your printout with the key. If you find any errors, retrieve the document and correct the errors.

6.15 Exit the program if you have finished working or clear your screen and continue straight on to the next exercise.

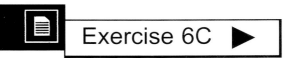

Exercise 6C ▶

6.16 Open a file and input the following text with an unjustified right margin:

> ### HISTORY OF ADVERTISING AND MEDIA GROWTH
>
> Advertising has been around for many centuries, and can be traced back to the days of ancient Greece, where historians found the first evidence of advertising being used for commercial purposes.
>
> The history of advertising and media growth can be traced across a number of centuries.
>
> During the 19th century, a number of factors combined to stimulate the growth of advertising in Britain. One of the most important was the development of large companies putting the mass output theories of Adam Smith into practice, and using economies of scale (buying raw materials in bulk at a cheaper price) to turn out huge amounts of goods at a lower unit price.

The first signs of media growth developed through printing in the second half of the 15th century which offered a whole new dimension. However, it was not until the end of the Industrial Revolution (late 18th century) that advertising began to really establish itself. By the 20th century a massive media growth was making its impact on society.

In order to maintain the output of such large quantities of food, soap, clothing and other items, these firms needed to develop mass consumption as well as mass output.

This led to the most important single medium for the communication of ideas, opinions, knowledge and advertisements - the newspaper. The newspaper was the first recognised modern mass medium.

6.17 Use the Spellcheck facility to check your work for spelling errors. Compare your work *on screen* with the printed text above. Proofread carefully and make any necessary amendments.

6.18 Save and print your document using filename **EX6C**. Check your printout with the printed exercise above. If you find any errors, make the necessary corrections.

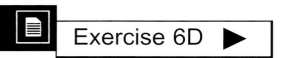 Exercise 6D ▶

6.19 Retrieve **EX6C** if it is not already on your screen.

6.20 In the first paragraph insert the word **clear** before **evidence**. In the last paragraph, insert the words **development of the** before **most important single medium**.

6.21 Delete the second paragraph beginning **The history of advertising ...**

6.22 Insert the following paragraph after the paragraph beginning **In order to maintain ...**

The best way of doing this, since they could not afford to employ enough salesmen to sell to the whole population in person, was by advertising.

6.23 In the paragraph beginning **During the 19th century ...**, insert **industrial** before **companies**. Replace **huge amounts** with **massive quantities**.

6.24 Reformat the document to

▶ justified right margin; and
▶ both margins insetted by 1.27 cm ($\frac{1}{2}$ in).

6.25 Move the paragraph beginning **The first signs of media ...** so it becomes the second paragraph in the document. Change the line spacing for this paragraph only to double-line spacing.

6.26 Replace the word **growth** with **expansion** throughout the document.

6.27 Centre and embolden the heading (and retain the underscore).

6.28 Save and print your document using filename **EX6D**. Check your printout with the key. If you find any errors, retrieve the document and correct the errors.

6.29 Exit the program if you have finished working or clear your screen and continue on to the next unit.

By the end of Unit 7, you should have learnt how to:

▶ amend typescript by inserting or deleting text as instructed
▶ expand correctly common abbreviations
▶ amend commonly misspelt words and their derivatives
▶ amend uncorrected typographical errors

Typescript containing correction signs ▶

A word processor operator is seldom given work which simply requires to be copied exactly as it is. A photocopier could do the job much more quickly! Usually, the 'copy' (text which the operator copies from) contains amendments.

Examples

> *amended*
> This sentence has been ~~changed~~.

should be keyed in as **This sentence has been amended**.

> Please delete ~~or omit~~ this word.

should be keyed in as **Please delete this word**.

> *this sentence*
> Extra words should be inserted for/to make sense.

should be keyed in as **Extra words should be inserted for this sentence to make sense**.

> You may be asked to move words or (sentences or) phrases.

should be keyed in as **You may be asked to move sentences or words or phrases**.

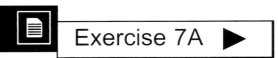
7.1 Starting a new file, key in the following text making all the necessary amendments as you go along:

ADMINISTRATIVE
~~ADMINISTRATION~~ WORK (Use double line-spacing)

Every organisation has to keep records and communicate. ~~Organisations~~ Businesses depend upon

each other for their success and the inefficiency of one can affect many others. Within

~~an organisation~~ a company, administrative workers are responsible for ensuring that all processes

run smoothly ~~and the product or service is supplied to the external customer~~. Each

individual within an organisation has internal customers - people or departments who

rely on them for information.

If you enjoy keeping things in order, planning your workload, and paying attention to

detail, you have the basic skills to become an administrator. Most of the work is carried out

indoors with the use of computers ~~so it may not be suitable work for someone who~~

~~likes to be out in the open air~~. You also need to be able to get on well with other

people, not just customers but your colleagues too. You can take pride in doing a job

well and providing efficient and vital support to the organisation which employs you.

Some administrative work is routine but, at a supervisory level, it becomes very

complex and requires a (mature) flexible attitude and the ability to make decisions

quickly. It is important to be observant and to enjoy meeting challenges.

7.2 Save your work using the filename **EX7A**. Do not close the file. Do not print your work at this stage. Press **Ctrl** + ↵ to start a new page.

Typescript containing abbreviations

Text authors often use abbreviations when writing out copy which is to be processed by a word processor operator. In the work situation, you would quickly get used to individual authors' 'shorthand'.

The following list shows some abbreviations you can expect to come across in basic examinations such as RSA's Initial Text Processing Skills:

info	**information**	**ref(d)**	**refer(red)**
necy	**necessary**	**ref(s)**	**reference(s)**
opp(s)	**opportunity/ies**	**sec(s)**	**secretary/ies**
org	**organisation**	**yr(s)**	**year(s)**
poss	**possible**	**yr(s)**	**your(s)**

Some abbreviations should be kept, for example:

etc	**eg**	**ie**	**NB**
PS	**plc**	**Ltd**	**& (in company names)**

Note: In the RSA examinations, there are no 'full stops' after the above abbreviations.

TIP: Word's spelling check may suggest that some abbreviations such as ie and eg should have full stops, for example i.e. and e.g. You can add the desired version to the spelling memory. Key in the abbreviations and run spelling check. When the checker stops on the abbreviation, click the **Add** button. Word will then add this to its memory and will not suggest full stops in this abbreviation again.

You will also be expected to key in the following in full.

▶ Days of the week, eg Wednesday, Thursday.
▶ Months of the year, eg February, September.
▶ Words in addresses, eg Grove, Drive, Crescent.
▶ Complimentary closes, eg Yours faithfully/sincerely.

Don't forget that you should use the Spelling tool before you save and print each document.

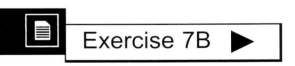 # Exercise 7B ▶

7.3   Key in the following text, using double-line spacing and typing all the abbreviations in full as you go along:

It is poss that when you apply for a post as a sec, you may find it necy to obtain a ref from a previous employer or from yr College tutor. Any org which is recruiting new staff will take every opp to find out as much as poss about prospective candidates.

A ref will provide valuable info on yr skills and abilities and, if you have just left College, the Personnel Department may ref to yr tutor for details of yr previous yr's work. Yr examination successes will show yr achievements, ie passes or distinctions in word processing, info technology etc.

7.4 Proofread your work carefully, comparing it with the printout in the key. If you find any errors, correct them. Use the Spelling tool to check that you have expanded the abbreviations correctly.

7.5 Save your document using the filename **EX7B** and print one copy. (Exercises 7A and 7B will be printed on separate sheets.)

 # Commonly misspelt words

Some words, although they are used frequently, are often spelt wrongly. It is up to you to get them right – fortunately, you have Word's Spelling tool to help you. In RSA's Initial Text Processing examination any words which are spelt wrongly in the draft will be circled.

The following list shows the words you may find in this examination:

accommodate	accommodates	accommodated	accommodating	accommodation
advertise	advertises	advertised	advertising	advertisement(s)
believe	believes	believed	believing	believable
business	businesses			
definite	definitely			
develop	develops	developed	developing	development
receive	receives	received	receiving	
recommend	recommends	recommended	recommending	recommendation
through				

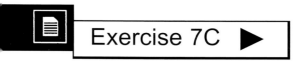

Exercise 7C ▶

7.6 Key in the following exercise, amending the circled words by referring to the list. Before printing, use Word's Spelling tool to check your work.

A group of local (buisness) owners has recently made (definate) plans for the (developement) of a new (busines) park in the town. They (beleive) that there is an increasing need for a complex of this type and have researched sites where such a (devellopment) could be (accomodated) After looking (though) the (advertisments) of specialist consultants, they have (definately) decided to employ a team of experts who they (belief) will be able to continue this research. In the near future, they hope to (recieve) the (recommendatins) of this team.

In (recomending) a particular site, the consultants have been requested to (develope) the idea of incorporating a hotel and leisure (bussiness,) which could offer (acommodation) for visiting (buisness) people and also for tourists. As the town is located on the fringes of a national park, the group (believs) that (biusness) and leisure interests can be (developped) together and each would receive benefit (throught) the activities and (advertiseing) of the other.

7.7 Format the document as follows:

▶ justified right margin;
▶ left and right margins of 3.17 cm or $1\frac{1}{4}$ in; and
▶ single-line spacing.

7.8 Save your work using the filename **EX7C**. Do not close the file. There is no need to print at this stage.

Typescript containing typographical errors ▶

Text processing may involve putting right any mistakes made in previous printouts. Watch out for uncorrected spelling errors and transposition errors.

Examples

This sentance contains 3 speling errers.

should be keyed in as: **This *sentence* contains 3 *spelling errors*.**

This sentence contians 2 transpositoin errors.

should be keyed in as: **This sentence *contains* 2 *transposition errors*.**

In the RSA Initial Text Processing Skills examination, any words which are incorrect will be circled. It is up to you to decide what is wrong and to key in the word correctly.

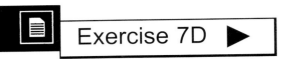

Exercise 7D ▶

7.9 Continuing in the same file, key in the following text, correcting all the words which are circled as you go along. Remember to expand abbreviations too. Use line spacing and margins as shown below.

HEALTH AND
/SAFETY AT WORK

When you fist start working for an org, you will take part in a induction program. In a small company, this may be carried out by yr immediate superior and be quiet informal. In a large org, you may join induction trainig along with other new employes.

You will be give info on risk assesment. You may have to submitt a reprot to the Health & Safety Representitive. It is the responsibility of both the employer and the the employee to ensure a safe working enviroment. Where more than 5 people are employed, it it necy to have a saftey policy and too implement it. Safety representatives form a Safety Commitee to monitor all aspects.

7.10 Proofread your work carefully, comparing it with the printout check in the key. If you find any errors, correct them. Use the Spelling tool to check that you have spelt the words correctly.

7.11 Save your document as **EX7D** and print one copy. (Exercises 7C and 7D will be printed on the same sheet.)

7.12 Exit the program if you have finished working or continue straight on to the next unit.

unit
8

▶ Checking text

By the end of Unit 8, you should have learnt how to:

▶ reproduce unfamiliar and foreign words correctly, copying the spelling exactly as shown

▶ amend uncorrected errors of agreement

▶ proofread your work carefully

 Text containing unfamiliar or foreign words

Each branch of commerce and each industry has its own vocabulary or 'jargon'.

It is vital that you take extra care when you are keying in words which are not familiar to you. If you come across a word which is new to you at work, note how it is spelt and copy it exactly, letter for letter. If you think the word is likely to crop up again, make a note of it. You should take particular care with the names of people or organisations, addresses, amounts of money, etc. It is a good idea to keep a note of regular contacts or clients.

Proofreading is very important with unfamiliar material. Check your work carefully yourself and, if possible, ask a colleague to check the work too. You could do the same for him or her!

Commonly used words can be added to the Spelling dictionary in Word so that they will be checked during the Spellcheck process. Don't forget to use the Spelling tool after each piece of work which you complete before you save and print.

 Exercise 8A

8.1 Starting a new file, key in the following text, copying the unfamiliar words carefully and expanding any abbreviations:

FACING THE INTERFACE

Technological innovation has revolutionised business systems and procedures. Jargon words have crept into our vocabulary although terms such as mainframe, laptop and Internet are generally understood nowadays. If you are required to become involved in

---

the purchase of computer hardware or software, you will have to undertake extensive research or ref to specialist consultants.

There are many factors to be considered when buying hardware: processing speed, memory size, pixels, peripherals etc. Operating systems programs such as Windows and OS/2 use a Graphical User Interface; DOS uses a textual interface. The icons you are learning to use in this book are examples of a Graphical User Interface. Fortunately, you do not have to know this to be able to use software such as Word for Windows!

Although you are inputting data into yr computer using the keyboard and the mouse, there are many other input devices such as bar-code readers, light pens, document readers and digitisers. Digitisers allow drawings and photographs to be displayed on a monitor.

8.2   Format the document as follows:

▶   justified margins;
▶   left and right margins of 3.8 cm or $1\frac{1}{2}$ in; and
▶   double spacing for whole document.

8.3   Save and print your work using the filename **EX8A**. Check your printout with the key. If you find any errors, correct them and save your document again. Print again if necessary.

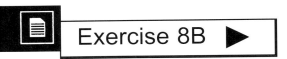

Exercise 8B ▶

8.4   Starting a new file, key in the following text, copying the unfamiliar words carefully and expanding any abbreviations:

MEETING TO COMMUNICATE

Organisations use meetings as a method of communicating between employees and with shareholders. The Articles of Association of a company may allow the Board of Directors to set up committees to perform certain tasks and then to report back to the Board. For example, an Advisory Committee could make recommendations but is not empowered to make binding decisions. A Standing Committee meets regularly and is a permanent group. Ad Hoc Committees are set up to achieve a particular purpose and then disbanded. Executive Committees have the power to make binding decisions within their terms of reference (intra vires).

Sometimes it is necy to form a Sub-Committee for a special purpose. A Joint Committee co-ordinates the work of other committees. Sub-Committees and Joint Committees may be 'standing' or 'ad hoc'.

Formal meetings must be quorate, ie the minimum number of members (the quorum) must be present. Proposals put to the meeting are usually called 'motions'. After discussion, a resolution is passed by voting. The Chairperson can discontinue (adjourn) a meeting and, if no date is set for its continuance, the adjournment is said to be 'sine die'.

8.5 Format the document as follows:

- ▶ ragged right margin;
- ▶ left and right margins of 4.4 cm or $1\frac{3}{4}$ in; and
- ▶ double spacing for last paragraph only.

8.6 Save and print your work using the filename **EX8B**. Check your printout with the key. If you find any errors, correct them and save your document again. Print again if necessary.

Typescript containing errors of agreement ▶

As you are keying in text, you should make sure that what you are typing makes sense. You should watch out for errors of agreement when the noun and the verb in a sentence do not agree.

Examples

> This class of girls are irritating.

should be keyed in as **This class of girls is irritating** (because there is only *one* class). If there were more than one class, you would key in: **These classes of girls are irritating**.

> The difference between the two word-processing programs were demonstrated by the supervisor

should be keyed in as **The difference between the two word-processing programs was demonstrated by the supervisor** (because there are *two* programs but only *one* difference).

Grammar tool

You learned in Unit 4 that Word 97 will check your document for possible grammar and style errors and offer suggestions for correcting them. If you know your grammar is weak, this is a useful facility, but still does not replace personal proofreading skills.

The grammar check facility should be used with caution since it may prompt you to make significant changes to another author's copy. This may not be acceptable to the text author. Changes of that nature should *not* be used when copying from an examination paper, when the copy must be followed exactly.

Exercise 8C ▶

8.7 Starting a new file, key in the following text – *retain all the deliberate grammatical mistakes* (these have been circled) for the purpose of this exercise.

E-MAIL MESSAGING

Reports, memos and letters prepared on a PC can be transmitted to another PC through electronic mail- the 'mailbox' system. The mailbox keep your messages in storage for you until you want to read them. If necessary , you can print out messages and file them or distribute them. The Internet allow any organisation to communicate with other users throughout the world, and are fast becoming the most popular method of using E-mail.

8.8   Move the cursor to the top of the file and select the spelling and grammar checking facility from the Tools menu or click the Spelling and Grammar icon on the Standard Tool Bar (unless automatic spelling and grammar check is already on). The Spelling and Grammar dialogue box appears on screen:

▶   Spelling and Grammar prompts you to consider whether the **comma** after **Reports** in the first line contributes to the clarity of the sentence. Imagine the sentence without the comma. In this case, it is clear that the comma is definitely needed for the sentence to make sense. Select **Ignore** from the dialogue box.

▶   Spelling and Grammar stops at the beginning of the second sentence because the subject and verb do not agree. The suggestions made are 'mailbox keeps' or 'mailboxes keep'. Ensure that **mailbox keeps** is highlighted and then select **Change** from the dialogue box.

▶   Spelling and Grammar stops at the beginning of the third sentence and points out that there is a space after the word **necessary** and before the **comma**. No space should be left before punctuation marks. Select **Change** from the dialogue box.

▶   Spelling and Grammar stops at the beginning of the fourth sentence because the subject and verb do not agree. The suggestion made is 'The Internet allows'. Select **Change** from the dialogue box.

▶   There is an error in the first sentence which Spelling and Grammar may not find. The **dash*** after the word **mail** should have one space before and after the symbol, e.g. **mail – the**. Insert this space yourself.

    *Note: The keyboard symbol for a dash and a hyphen is the same. A *dash* has *one space at each side of the symbol* and is used to separate words or to break up a sentence into clauses. A *hyphen* has *no spaces at each side of the symbol* and is used to join words together (e.g. mother-in-law). If you are not sure whether to use a dash or a hyphen, think about the effect you want to produce – are you joining words together or separating them?

▶   There is an error in the last sentence which Spelling and Grammar may not find. The last phrase should read **and *is* fast becoming the ... Change** this word yourself.

Remember, spelling and grammar checks are not sufficient on their own. You must check your work thoroughly too!

8.9   Close this file *without* saving.

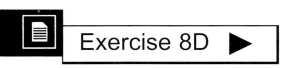

Exercise 8D ▶

8.10   Key in the following text correcting the circled words as you go along. Use line spacing and margin format as shown below.

FOLLOWING HOUSE STYLE ← *(Heading in bold please)*

When you start working for a new organisation, you may have to make amendments to the way in which you have previously prepared documents. Most companies have adopted a 'house style' for its documents, particularly letters. This ensures that there is a uniform presentation style for everything that leave the office.

If you are not sure of the house style, look in the files or folders you are using. You should find copies of documents previously used. In most cases, you will find that there is a 'template' on your word processor. You can simply retrieve this and enter the details in the appropriate places. The use of templates save a considerable amount of time as well as ensuring uniformity.

The style of presentation may be different from what you have learned and you may not like it but it may have been designed for a specific purposes and you will have to adopt the house style or your work will not be usable.

8.11 Proofread your work carefully, comparing it with the printout check in the key. If you find any errors, correct them. Use the Spelling and Grammar tool to check that you have amended the text correctly.

8.12 Save your work as **EX8D**. There is no need to print at this stage.

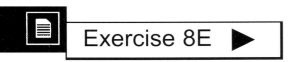

Exercise 8E ▶

8.13 Starting with **EX8D** on your screen, key in the following exercise below it. Key in the text as shown below (including words spelt incorrectly), but expanding abbreviations as you go along. Notice how Word identifies keying-in errors as you make them!

BUSINESS EXHIBITION ← *(Underline heading please)*

On Wed of next week, we intend to follow yr advise and take the opp of visiting the exhibition you recomended in our discussions last yr. We have advertise our org in many buisness publicatins, giving info on the development of our products in all poss areas.

Yr org have encouraged us to beleive in the power of advertiseing and we have made a definate committment to promoting our high-quality accomodation in this country and abroad. We hope to recceive positive feedback from our secs who will be enjoy the oportunity of meeting poss future customers at the exhibition.

8.14 Save and print your work using filename **EX8E**. Check your printout with the key. If you find any errors, correct them and save your document again. Print again if necessary.

8.15 Exit the program if you have finished working or continue straight on to the next unit.

unit

9

► Working from manuscript copy

By the end of Unit 9, you should have:

► practised keying in text from hand-written copy which contains amendments and corrections

► produced a notice from a hand-written draft

Typing from manuscript copy ►

'Manuscript' means written by hand. Word processor operators are often given work in hand-written form. When keying in from a hand-written draft, make sure you can read *all* the words. If any words are not clear, *look for the same letter formations* in other parts of the draft where they may be more legible. If you still have difficulty, read the document for context to try to get the sense of it. If you are still not sure, ask for help – but not in examinations of course!

The standard correction signs and abbreviations which you learned in Unit 7 will appear in manuscript copy as well as in typescript. Words in the text which are circled should be corrected as before.

Exercise 9A ►

9.1   Key in the following text, using a ragged right margin and double-line spacing:

TRANSPORT IN THE INDUSTRIAL REVOLUTION ← underline

The Industrial Revolution (increased) greatly↑ the demand (at the time) for coal, iron and other raw materials. Roads ✓ were often little more than rutted tracks – not suitable for the transportation of goods in bulk. The eighteenth century saw the building of canals across the country. This method of ~~moving~~ carrying goods, still using horse-drawn vessels, (were) usually faster than by roads.

The use of water ~~coarses~~ courses was not a new idea. The Romans, Chinese and Persians ~~all~~ also used canals.

The working life of the canals was rather short as railways provided a much ~~faster~~ swifter method of moving raw materials and manufactured goods. Railways began to be built in the ~~later~~ latter half of the 19th nineteenth century, & canals are now used more for leisure than for (buisness)

9.2 Use the Spelling tool and then proofread your work carefully comparing it with the printout check in the key. If you find any errors, correct them.

9.3 Save your work using the filename **EX9A** and print one copy.

 Exercise 9B ▶

9.4 Key in the following text, using a justified right margin throughout and double-line spacing for the first paragraph only:

New Appointments ← (embolden heading)

recent
The / major review of our org has identified a (definate) need to recruit more administrators. The increase in our sales and customer service functions (mean) that it will be necy to appoint new / people for our Call Centre.

practise
The persons appointed should ~~have~~ an efficient way of working and possess / excellent ~~interpersonal~~ communication skills. Companies are judged by first impressions & by the after-sales service they provide. A courteous response and prompt action by individuals empowered to deal with problems are both factors which (leads) to satisfied customers.

We have made preliminary arrangements for the training of staff by a specialist team. Product knowledge will be extensively covered by our own Company trainers during ~~the~~ induction sessions.

Our Human Resource Manager, with the help of colleagues in the Customer Service Department, (are) currently working on press (advertisments.)

9.5   Proofread your work carefully, using the Spelling tool.

9.6   Save and print your document using the filename **EX9B**. Check your printout with the key. If you find any errors, correct them.

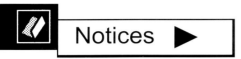

Notices ▶

You may be asked to produce a notice to be displayed on a bulletin board or to be sent out to customers or members. An eye-catching and informative notice should be well displayed and should not contain too much information.

You could use all the text-formatting functions available on Word 97, including graphics. However, for the purposes of the RSA Initial Text Processing examination, you are required to use only the text emphasis methods you learned in Unit 5. You should still key in the text as shown, copying capitalisation, not changing the word order, and not omitting or adding words.

You may want to centre the text and to insert more clear lines between the lines of text to make the notice easier to read.

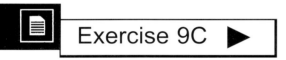

Exercise 9C ▶

9.7   Key in the following notice, copying the text as shown, but adding text emphasis to create an attractive display:

> CANALS – PAST AND PRESENT
>
> A talk by Dr James Arkwright
> of the STATON CIVIC TRUST
>
> Tickets £2.00   Concessions £1.50
> Book at Staton Library or Post Office
>
> STATON CIVIC CENTRE
>
> Mon 25 Apr
> 8 pm
>
> Refreshments
>
> BOOK EARLY – TICKETS ARE LIMITED

9.8   Proofread your work carefully, using the Spelling tool.

9.9   Save and print your document using the filename **EX9C**. Check your printout with the key. If you find any errors in the text, correct them. Your display may be different from the one shown in the printout check; this does not mean that yours is wrong.

9.10   Exit the program if you have finished working or continue straight on to the next unit.

► Producing a personal business letter

By the end of Unit 10, you should have learnt how to:

► complete a personal business letter
► insert a new page break

Note: Although Word 97 has an in-built Letter Wizard facility, it is not entirely suitable for RSA examination purposes.

Producing a personal business letter
(using the 'fully blocked' style with open punctuation) ►

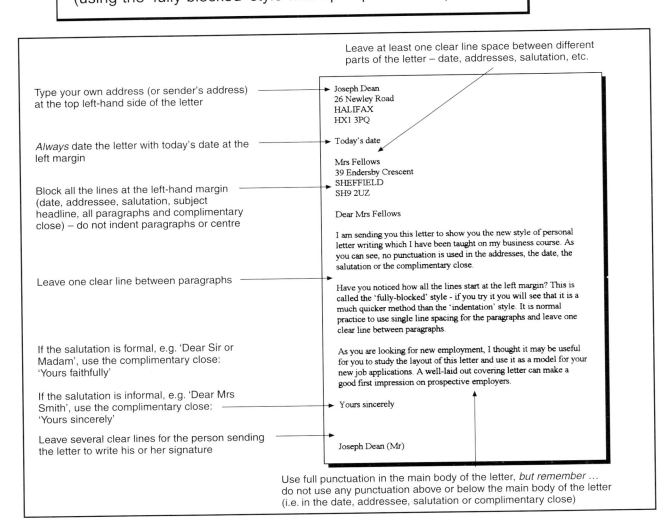

Leave at least one clear line space between different parts of the letter – date, addresses, salutation, etc.

Type your own address (or sender's address) at the top left-hand side of the letter

Joseph Dean
26 Newley Road
HALIFAX
HX1 3PQ

Always date the letter with today's date at the left margin

Today's date

Block all the lines at the left-hand margin (date, addressee, salutation, subject headline, all paragraphs and complimentary close) – do not indent paragraphs or centre

Mrs Fellows
39 Endersby Crescent
SHEFFIELD
SH9 2UZ

Dear Mrs Fellows

I am sending you this letter to show you the new style of personal letter writing which I have been taught on my business course. As you can see, no punctuation is used in the addresses, the date, the salutation or the complimentary close.

Leave one clear line between paragraphs

Have you noticed how all the lines start at the left margin? This is called the 'fully-blocked' style - if you try it you will see that it is a much quicker method than the 'indentation' style. It is normal practice to use single line spacing for the paragraphs and leave one clear line between paragraphs.

As you are looking for new employment, I thought it may be useful for you to study the layout of this letter and use it as a model for your new job applications. A well-laid out covering letter can make a good first impression on prospective employers.

If the salutation is formal, e.g. 'Dear Sir or Madam', use the complimentary close: 'Yours faithfully'

If the salutation is informal, e.g. 'Dear Mrs Smith', use the complimentary close: 'Yours sincerely'

Yours sincerely

Leave several clear lines for the person sending the letter to write his or her signature

Joseph Dean (Mr)

Use full punctuation in the main body of the letter, *but remember* ... do not use any punctuation above or below the main body of the letter (i.e. in the date, addressee, salutation or complimentary close)

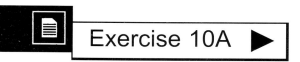

10.1 Key in the letter shown below – follow the layout of the letter as shown but allow Word's wordwrap to make the line endings. There is no need for you to type the instructions shown in the margin – they are simply a guide to help you identify the different parts of a letter.

10.2 Save your document using filename **EX10A**. Check your work carefully on screen. You do not need to print out your work at this stage.

Joseph Dean
26 Newley Road
HALIFAX
HX1 3PQ
Leave one clear line
Today's date
Leave one clear line
Mrs Fellows
39 Endersby Crescent
SHEFFIELD
SH9 2UZ
Leave one clear line
Dear Mrs Fellows
Leave one clear line

I am sending you this letter to show you the new style of personal letter writing which I have been taught on my business course. As you can see, no punctuation is used in the addresses, the date, the salutation or the complimentary close. (Punctuation is only used in the body of the letter to make sure that it makes sense.)

Leave one clear line

Have you noticed how all the lines start at the left margin? This is called the 'fully blocked' style - if you try it you will see that it is a much quicker method than the 'indentation' style. It is normal practice to use single line-spacing for the paragraphs and leave one clear line between paragraphs.

Leave one clear line

As you are looking for new employment, I thought it may be useful for you to study the layout of this letter and use it as a model for your new job applications. A well laid out covering letter can make a good first impression on prospective employers.

Leave one clear line
Yours sincerely
Leave five clear lines

Joseph Dean (Mr)

Margin annotations:
- *address of sender*
- *date in full*
- *name and address of addressee (i.e. person you are sending the letter to)*
- *salutation*
- *main body of letter*
- *complimentary close*
- *space for signature*
- *name of signatory (sender)*

10.3 With document **EX10A** still on screen, position the cursor at the end of the document and insert a new page break so that you will be able to key in a new letter on a separate page.

Insert a new page break ▶

When keying in a long document, Word automatically inserts page breaks for you. These are called 'soft' page breaks. You can choose to insert a page break yourself whenever you want to start a new page – eg the start of a new chapter. This is called a 'manual' or 'hard' page break.

Keyboard	Mouse and menu
Position cursor where you want to insert the page break:	
Press: **Ctrl + ↵** (Return)	Select: **Insert, Break, Page Break, OK**

 ## Exercise 10B ▶

10.4 At the start of the second page, key in the following document from the manuscript draft:

The Ebony Club
45 Marton Cres
WAKEFIELD
WF5 3RT

Mary Wadsworth
12 New St
WAKEFIELD
WF4 9EW

Dear Mary

I am writing to thank you for yr excellent presentation ⟨at the Ebony Club⟩ last Thurs evening.

I have ⟨recieved⟩ ⟨several⟩ several requests from our committee enquiring if it would be poss for you to make a ✦visit ⟨return⟩ in about six months' time when we will
be holding our ^annual /open evening. ⟨when this becomes available⟩

I will forward more info about the evening. The date for your diary is 16 Oct 1998 – we shall probably begin ^around [8.00pm.

Could you please let my sec have yr bank details so that we can settle your fee in full? ⟨payment⟩ will be made according to our agreed rate.

I have ⟨reccommended⟩ you to several other orgs ~~which~~ that I ⟨beleive⟩ would benefit from yr services.

Yrs sncly
Steven Bentley (Mr)

10.5   Save the file using the filename **EX10B**. Use the print preview facility to check that the layout of your letters is correct, then print the file **EX10B**. The letter you completed as Exercise 10A will also be printed. Check your printouts with the key. If you find any errors, make the necessary corrections. Keep your printout of the first letter (**EX10A**) for future reference on correct letter layout.

10.6   Exit the program if you have finished working or continue straight on to the next unit.

unit 11

▶ Examination Practice 2

By the end of Unit 11, you should have completed a mock examination for the RSA Initial Text Processing Award.

 RSA Initial Text Processing

The Initial Text Processing examination assesses your ability to produce simple documents such as a letter, a notice and a short article from hand-written and type-written draft. The award demonstrates that you have acquired basic skills in word processing (or typewriting).

The examination lasts for one hour and you have to complete three documents. Printing is done outside this time.

Examinations are carried out in registered centres and are marked by RSA examiners. The centre will provide A4 plain paper.

Examination hints

When sitting your examination:

▶ you may use a manual prepared by the centre or the software manufacturer;

▶ put your name, centre number and document number on each document;

▶ check your work very carefully before printing – proofread, spell check; and

▶ assemble your printouts in the correct order at the end of the examination.

You are now ready to try a mock examination for Initial Text Processing. Take care and good luck!

The list of assessment criteria for this examination is long and detailed. To be sure that you have reached the required standard to be entered for an examination, you need to work through several past papers and have these 'marked' by a tutor or assessor who is qualified and experienced in this field.

Results

▶ If your finished work has 15 faults or fewer, you will be awarded a **distinction**.

▶ If your finished work has between 16 and 30 faults, you will be awarded a **pass**.

Results are sent to the centre where you sit your examination.

Worth House
Aire St
STATON
N Yorkshire
NY6 3GE

Miss J M Pinfold
3 Derby Rd
STATON
N Yorkshire
NY12 4LD

Dear Miss Pinfold

Thank you for returning the membership application form.

I understand that you are interested in ~~being~~ becoming a full member of the Association and I am pleased ~~to be able~~ to confirm that yr refs have been checked by our (comittee) and ~~have~~ (they) given their approval to your application.

Please ~~forward~~ let us have yr cheque for the annual subscription fee (to the Association) of £30. This should be sent to Mrs C Rollinson, Sec at the above address.

Our ~~Monthly~~ meetings are held at Worth House, Aire St, on the second Thurs of each month. A full programme giving info on speakers and visits will be sent to you as soon as poss.

I would like to take this opp to welcome you to the Association and hope that you will enjoy our activities.

Yrs sncly

Rosemary Caton

(Filename: EX11DOC1)

(Notice)

ASSOCIATION OF PERSONAL ASSISTANTS

Visit to Head Office of
the STATON & WOODFORD TIMES

Thurs 12th Mar at 7.00 pm

Tour of new premises
Talk by Miss B Bridge, Sec to Editor
Presentation: Technology in Journalism Today

Buffet supper provided

Meet at Woodford House, Staton Rd, Woodford
at 6.45 pm

(Filename: EX11DOC2)

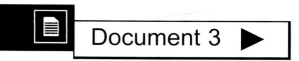

Document 3 ►

Please retype this article. Make amendments as shown; correct circled words.

ORGANISING YOUR WORKSTATION

Whether your working office is large and open-plan or small & private, it (need) to be organised so that you can work efficiently and comfortably. The furniture ~~itself~~ may be (our) of yr control but it may be poss to suggest improvements when the right time comes along!

~~Your desk is probably home to a computer terminal with keyboard and mouse, telephone and other items such as paper and writing implements.~~ Try to keep the desk surface as tidy as possible so that you can spread out when you need to do written work. Secs should use a copy-holder when ~~you~~ *they* are keying in and make sure that ~~she~~ *they* (sits) properly on a well-designed chair.

~~If you get into the habit of filing papers regularly and dealing with documents as they come to you, you will accumulate less clutter.~~ (Develope) the habit of placing loose papers in folders with a (definate) label such as 'To do' or 'To read'. It may not be poss to handle each (doucment) only once as some (buisness) managers (recomend) but ~~this~~ *the* strategy *of using folders* (reduce) the risk of losing papers.

If you are organised,
/Y*y*ou will then be able to locate info necy for yr job. Anyone looking at your desk and working areas will feel that you are efficient and a credit to yr org. Some people (beleive) that a tidy desk shows a tidy mind!

(Filename: EX11DOC3)

unit
12

► Rearranging and editing text

By the end of Unit 12, you should have learnt how to:

► amend typescript by using common correction signs as instructed
► expand correctly additional common abbreviations
► amend additional commonly misspelt words and their derivatives
► rearrange text as instructed

 ## Typescript containing correction signs ►

In Unit 7, you learned basic text amendment techniques. In this unit, you will learn additional correction signs. The following list shows some correction signs you can expect to come across in elementary examinations such as RSA's Text Processing Stage I Parts 1 and 2:

Correction sign	Meaning
[or //	Start a new paragraph here.
	Run on – join paragraphs or sections of text.
	Transpose horizontally.
	Transpose vertically.
✓ word	Let it be. Key in or retain the word(s) with the dashed underline.

Examples and method

Before amendment

To insert a new paragraph when amending existing text, place the cursor or I-beam immediately before the first character of what will be the second paragraph.[Then press the ↵ (return or enter) key twice to create one clear line between the two paragraphs.

After amendment

To insert a new paragraph when amending existing text, place the cursor or I-beam immediately before the first character of what will be the second paragraph.

Then press the ↵ (return or enter) key twice to create one clear line between the two paragraphs.

To join two paragraphs or blocks of text into one, place the cursor or I-beam immediately before the first character of the second paragraph. Then press the ← (backspace delete) key twice to delete the space. Adjust spacing after punctuation if necessary.

To join two paragraphs or blocks of text into one, place the cursor or I-beam immediately before the first character of the second paragraph. Then press the ← (backspace delete) key twice to delete the space. Adjust spacing after punctuation if necessary.

To transpose two words adjacent in the same sentence, select one word and then move the mouse pointer onto the word (an 'open' white 'arrow' should appear). Holding down the mouse left button, drag and drop the word into its new position.

To transpose two adjacent words in the same sentence, select one word and then move the mouse pointer onto the word (an 'open' white 'arrow' should appear). Holding down the left mouse button, drag and drop the word into its new position.

To transpose words in a list, select one word and, using the open arrow below the text selected, drag and drop the word into its new position. Repeat with other words as necessary

Dot Matrix
Laser
Ink Jet
Thermal

Dot Matrix
Ink Jet
Laser
Thermal

---

deleted
When you see crossed out words with a line of dashes underneath one of them and a tick inside a circle in the margin, this means that you should use the word with the dotted underline and not the other word.

When you see deleted words with a line of dashes underneath one of them and a tick inside a circle in the margin, this means that you should use the word with the dashed underline and not the other word.

Exercise 12A ▶

12.1 Starting a new file, key in the following text making all the necessary amendments as you go along:

Who Does What? ← (CAPS and underline heading please)

internal

A company's org chart shows the / structure and lines of responsibility. The chart looks rather like a family tree and shows usually a hierarchical structure. The span of control of individual managers sets out the person to whom each employee is responsible. It is important that the chart both stipulates and reflects effective lines of communication within a company.

Many problems are caused by poor or inadequate communications procedures. //Another vital document for employees is the job description - their own & other people's. This should clearly outline the following info:

→ (Department)
↳ (Job Title)
→ Objectives
→ Person(s) accountable for
→ Person(s) accountable to
→ (Responsibilities)

Single line-spacing throughout document please

 The job description is ~~normally~~ usually sent to prospective applicants, together with a person specification which gives details of qualifications, skills and qualities considered essential or desirable for the postholder. Applicants should (match carefully) their own capabilities with the ∧specification.
(person)

12.2 Save your work as **EX12A**. There is no need to print at this stage.

◀ Typescript containing abbreviations ▶

Text authors often use abbreviations when writing out copy which is to be processed by a word processor operator. In the work situation, you would quickly get used to individual authors' 'shorthand'.

Look back at Unit 7 to refresh your memory on the abbreviations you learned there. The following list shows some extra abbreviations you can expect to come across in elementary examinations such as RSA's Text Processing Stage I Parts 1 and 2:

a/c(s)	account(s)	**dr**	dear
approx	approximately	**misc**	miscellaneous
cat(s)	catalogue(s)	**sig(s)**	signature(s)
co(s)	company(ies)	**temp**	temporary

Remember
As you learned in Unit 7, some abbreviations should be kept, for example:

etc	**eg**	**ie**	**NB**
PS	**plc**	**Ltd**	**& (in company names)**

Note: In the RSA examination, there are no 'full stops' after the above abbreviations.

You will also be expected to key in the following in full:

▶ Days of the week, eg Wednesday, Thursday.
▶ Months of the year, eg February, September.
▶ Words in addresses, eg Grove, Drive, Crescent.
▶ Complimentary closes, eg Yours faithfully/sincerely.

Don't forget that you should use the Spelling tool before you save and print each document.

Exercise 12B ▶

12.3 Retrieve **EX12A** and key in the following text below the previous text, typing all the abbreviations in full as you go along:

> lay the foundations
> Job descriptions and org charts ~~are a basis~~ for
> ensuring good communications and efficient
> operations. All employees need to take a/c of
> the co's published documents, eg policies on
> equal opps, health and safety etc as these
> ✓ help to ~~decide~~ determine each |individual| employee's|
> role and responsibilities, in addition to those ↑
> shown in their job description.
> (relating to the specific)
> post

12.4 Proofread your work carefully, comparing it with the printout check in the key. If you find any errors, correct them. Use the Spelling tool to check that you have expanded the abbreviations correctly.

12.5 Save your document using the filename **EX12B** and print one copy.

Commonly misspelt words ▶

Some words, although they are used frequently, are often spelt wrongly. It is up to you to get them right – fortunately, you have Word 97's Spelling tool to help you. Look back at Unit 7 to refresh your memory on the commonly misspelt words you learned there.

The following list shows some extra words you can expect to come across in elementary examinations such as RSA's Text Processing Stage I Parts 1 and 2:

acknowledge	**foreign**
appreciate	**government**
client	**inconvenient**
colleague	**receipt**
committee	**responsible**

correspondence   separate

expense   sufficient

experience   temporary

financial

Derivatives of the above words

In RSA examinations, you will also be expected to spell correctly any derivatives of the above words such as plurals, past tense, etc. Examples are colleagues, acknowledged, appreciating, separation.

If any of the above words are incorrect in the examination draft, they will be circled. It is up to you to identify what is wrong and make sure the text is correct.

Exercise 12C ▶

12.6   Key in the following exercise, amending the circled words by referring to the previous list. Before printing, use the Spelling tool to check your work.

Making application ← *CAPS and centre heading*

The letter

As with any correspondance for which you are responsable, yr letter of application should show that you apprecate the need for good presentation and complete accuracy. Do not add yr sig to a letter if it it not sufficently good. Signing a letter makes you responsiblej for its content.

The advertisment in the newspaper probably requested good buisness and administrative skills such as checking and proof-reading!

On receit of letters of application, experenced personnel assess them, seperating some to draw up a 'short list' of approx six applicants who are judged to have sufficiant necy experience for the post advertised.

Unfortunately, some cos do not ~~acknowledge~~ send any acknowledgment to unsuccessful applicants, perhaps because the financal expence is great. ~~However,~~ Applicants are left waitiing for correspondance having gone to the exspense of submitting an application. Applying for even one post take a considerable amount of time. It can be inconveniant when applicants are in the position of having to make a definate decision about taking a post without having info on other applications they have made.

Additional info

A letter of application may need a separate application form or curriculum vitae. Specific info may be requested, eg

Work history - (tempory) and permanent posts held
(Experence) of liaising with (clients) and (colleages)
(Foriegn) language competence
Qualifications and attainments
Education

You may sometimes see that an (advetisement) (inform) applicants that they should
assume they have been unsuccessful if they have not heard from the co within a given
period of time.

12.7 Save and print your work using the filename **EX12C**. Proofread your work carefully, comparing it with
the printout check in the key. If you find any errors, correct them.

Rearranging text in a document ▶

One of the most useful facilities of word processing is the ability to rearrange text on the screen and
then print the document when all the changes have been made. The first draft is sent to the author of
the text who marks up the print the document to show what changes are needed. The word
processor operator can recall the document from disk, edit the text and then print out the final copy.

Rearrangement of text is part of elementary text processing examinations. Look back at Unit 2 to
refresh your memory on moving blocks of text.

Exercise 12D ▶

12.8 Retrieve EX12B and amend the text as shown below, rearranging the paragraphs as shown:

WHO DOES WHAT?

the
A company's organisation chart shows internal structure and lines of responsibility.
The chart looks rather like a family tree and usually shows a hierarchical structure.

The span of control of individual managers sets out the person to whom each _directs_
employee is responsible. It is important that the chart both stipulates and reflects
effective lines of communication within a company. Many problems are caused by
poor or inadequate communications procedures.

⊘ Another vital document for employees is the job description - their own and other‸s. people's. This should clearly outline the following information:

Job Title
Department
Objectives
Responsibilities
(Person(s) accountable for)
(Person(s) accountable to)

The job description is normally sent to prospective applicants, together with a ~~person~~ *job* specification which gives details of qualifications, skills and qualities considered essential or desirable for the postholder. Applicants should carefully match their own capabilities with the ~~person~~ *job* specification.

~~Job descriptions and~~ **O**rganisation charts lay the foundations for ensuring good communications and efficient operations. All employees need to take account of the company's published documents, eg policies on equal opportunities, health and safety etc as these help to determine each employee's individual role and responsibilities, in addition to those relating to ~~the~~ *their* specific post ~~shown in their job description~~.

12.9 Proofread your work carefully, comparing it with the printout check in the key. If you find any errors, correct them

12.10 Save your document as **EX12D** and print one copy

 Exercise 12E ▶

12.11 Retrieve **EX12C** and amend the text as shown below, rearranging paragraphs as shown.

MAKING ‸*A JOB* APPLICATION

<u>The letter</u>

(of an acceptable standard)

As with any correspondence for which you are responsible, your letter of application should show that you appreciate the need for good presentation and complete accuracy. Do not add your signature to a letter if it is not ~~sufficiently good~~. Signing a letter makes you responsible for its content. The advertisement in the newspaper probably requested good business and administrative skills such as checking and proof-reading!

On receipt of letters of application, experienced personnel assess them, separating some to draw up a 'short list' of approximately six applicants who are judged to have sufficient necessary experience for the advertised post.

Unfortunately, some companies do not send any acknowledgement to unsuccessful applicants, perhaps because the financial expense is great. Applicants are left waiting for correspondence, having gone to the expense of submitting an application. Applying for even one post takes a considerable amount of time. It can be inconvenient when applicants are in the position of having to make a definite decision about taking a post without having ~~information~~ feedback on other applications they have made.

Additional information

A letter of application may need a separate application form or curriculum vitae. Specific information may be requested, eg

Work history - temporary and permanent posts held
Experience of liaising with clients and colleagues
Foreign language competence
Qualifications and attainments
Education

You may sometimes see that an advertisement informs applicants that they should assume they have been unsuccessful if they have not heard from the company within a given period of time.

12.12 Proofread your work carefully, comparing it with the printout check in the key. If you find any errors, correct them.

12.13 Save your document as **EX12E** and print one copy.

12.14 Exit the program if you have finished working or continue straight on to the next unit.

▶ Producing a memorandum

By the end of Unit 13, you should have learnt how to:

▶ complete a memorandum

▶ use a preprinted form or template file

▶ use the Tab key to line up text

Memorandum layout ▶

A memorandum is a document sent 'internally' to convey information to people who work in the same organisation.

At the top of the document, it is customary to enter **From** whom the document is being sent, **To** whom it is being sent, and to include a **Reference**, the **Date** of sending and usually a **Subject Heading**. There is no complimentary close.

You should always insert the date, even if there are no specific instructions to do so – this will be expected of you in the RSA examination. Some people like to sign or initial their memos but this is not absolutely necessary.

Organisations have different ways of aligning and setting out the items on the memo. Two acceptable versions are shown in Figure 13.1.

Using a template file

Templates are often used in business to give a consistent look to the company's documents. A template is a blueprint for specific text, graphics and formatting which will always appear in a document.

JAMES DALTON ENGINEERING LTD
MEMORANDUM

From:	Sender	**Ref:**	AZ456
To:	Receiver	**Date:**	today's

SUBJECT HEADING

Study the layout and spacing of the top part of the memo carefully.

Type the body of the memo in single-line spacing with a clear line space between paragraphs.

JAMES DALTON ENGINEERING LTD
MEMORANDUM

From: Sender
To: Receiver
Ref: AZ456
Date: today's

Figure 13.1 Memorandum

Memos are a good example of template use as they contain the company name, standard headings, a date field and place holders to indicate where you type the text.

Word does have a set of templates that you can use as they are or adapt – however, these require saving in a different format. For the purposes of this book and the elementary examination requirements, therefore, you will save your template files in the normal way.

After retrieving your original template file, and keying in additional details, you should always ensure that you give the second document a *different* filename. This means that you will not 'overwrite' your template file and you will then be able to retrieve and use the template blueprint over and over again.

To create a template:

▶ Key in: Only those details you want to reappear every time you open the template file.
▶ Save: The file in the normal way as a Word document.
▶ Enter: Your filename for the template file.

To open/retrieve a template for use:

▶ Select: **Open** from the **File** menu.
▶ Open/retrieve: Your template file in the normal way.
▶ Select: **Save As** from the **File** menu.
▶ Enter: A **different filename** for your second document so that you don't overwrite your template blueprint.
▶ Add: The rest of the information to the template. For example, if you have retrieved a memohead, key in the rest of the details for the memo.

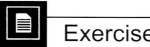

Exercise 13A ▶

13.1 You have already created a file that you can now use as a memohead template blueprint. Open the file you saved in Unit 5 under the filename **Memohead**.

13.2 The 'Better Business Services Ltd' template memo form should now appear on screen ready for you to complete with the rest of the details. Press: **Ctrl + End** to move the cursor to the end of the heading and press ↵ twice.

Important: Before keying in any additional details, you will need to reset the font to Times New Roman, point size 12. You will also need to alter the margin alignment and switch off bold and underline.

13.3 Locate the Tab key on your keyboard – this is sometimes labelled as $\overset{|\leftarrow}{\rightarrow|}$. In Word 97 the tab settings are normally defaulted (i.e. previously set) to every 13 mm ($\frac{1}{2}$ in). Each time you press the Tab key you indent the line by 13 mm ($\frac{1}{2}$ in). The Tab key is often used to align text – if you align text on screen by pressing the Space Bar it may not always line up when you print.

Select the **Save As** command from the **File** menu (so that you don't overwrite your memo template file). Use the filename **EX13A**.

Key in the rest of the memorandum from the copy shown below – use the **Tab** key to align the text after the memo headings **FROM**, **TO**, **REF** and **DATE**.

```
FROM:        Dave Mills, PREMISES MANAGER
TO:          Madeleine Yeats, PERSONNEL OFFICER
DATE:        today's
REF:         DM/011491
```

STAFF SHORTAGES

In relation to the brief discussion we had last ~~year~~ week about the ~~severe~~ shortage of ⟨are able to⟩ ⟨acommodation⟩ staff, I have now drafted a job description for the two temp positions which should alleviate the situation until we ↑recruit permanent staff.

I am still collecting all the info needed to assess how many permanent additional staff the org will need for necy maintenance standards. I would ⟨apreciate⟩ yr comments on appropriate salary scales before the end of next week, if poss. There may be an opp to discuss this issue at ~~the~~ our meeting tomorrow.

It would also be helpful if you could let me have a copy of the new salary scales which will come into force next year.

I have recd the draft induction policy for new staff which you circulated last week. I think it is ⟨definately⟩ a step in the right direction.

13.4   Save your document. Print your document then check your printout with the key. If you find any errors, retrieve the document and correct.

Using a preprinted form ▶

In Word the top margin is usually set by default to 2.54 cm (1 in). When printing on a preprinted form, the top margin on the first page only should be increased to accommodate the printed heading. (Second and subsequent pages are usually printed on plain paper.) You may need to measure the depth of the preprinted heading on the form you intend to use, and to experiment to find the top margin measurement required. Make sure you know how to insert headed paper into the paper feed tray of your printer so that the document is printed in the correct position.

Altering the top margin to leave space for a preprinted form heading
One-page documents

▶ Select: **Page Setup** from the **File** menu.
▶ Select: The **Margins** tab.
▶ In the **Top** box: Notice the default top margin is normally set at 2.54 cm (1 in) (Figure 13.2).
▶ To replace this with extra measurement needed, either select or overtype with the measurement required to leave sufficient space for the depth

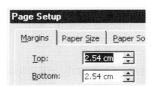

Figure 13.2

of the preprinted heading *plus* one or more clear line spaces (Figure 13.3) .

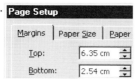

▶ Select: **Whole Document** from the **Apply to** box

; then click on **OK**.

Figure 13.3

Multi-page documents

▶ Repeat the above procedure: For the page on which you want to leave space for the preprinted form heading – usually Page 1. Then, to revert to a normal top margin for all subsequent pages:

▶ Position the cursor: At the *bottom* of the same page which carries the extra heading space:

▶ Select: **File**, **Page Setup**, **Margins**.

▶ In the **Top** box: select or key in: **2.54 cm** (**1 in**) – or alternative standard top margin measurement.

▶ Select: **This point forward** from the **Apply to** box; click on **OK**.

Note: This ensures that the increased top margin measurement is only set for the page with the preprinted heading on it – all other pages in the document follow standard top margin settings.

Exercise 13B ▶

13.5 If you are unable to access the printer or cannot use the preprinted form method for some other reason, ignore the following instructions and complete Exercise 13B in the same way as you completed Exercise 13A, using the template method. Otherwise, open the file you saved in Unit 5 as **Memohead**. Print out a copy. Measure the depth of the preprinted memo heading from the top of the page to the bottom of the heading text and allow for two or three clear line spaces after it. In total, this should be approximately 6.35 cm (2.5 in). You are going to print Exercise 13A directly on to this preprinted form in step 13.9. First:

13.6 Starting a new file, key in the memorandum details from the copy shown below following the amendments indicated. Press the **Tab** key to line up the text after the memo headings **FROM**, **TO**, **REF** and **DATE**.

13.7 Following the instructions given at the beginning of this unit, alter the Top Margin so that the body of the document does not 'overprint' on top of the preprinted memo heading. Remember that you will probably need to enter a setting of 6.35 cm (2.5 in) for the top margin in order to allow for several clear line spaces after the heading text.

13.8 Save your document using filename **EX13B**.

13.9 Insert the preprinted memo form (ie the document **Memohead** which you printed out at step 13.5) correctly into your printer. Print the document **EX13B** directly on to the memohead form. Check your printout with the key. If you find any errors, retrieve the document and correct the errors.

13.10 Exit the program if you have finished working or continue straight on to the next unit.

Better Business Services Ltd

MEMORANDUM

FROM: Madeleine Yeats, PERSONNEL OFFICER
TO: Dave Mills, PREMISES MANAGER
DATE: ~~today's~~
REF: MY/00ZA2

ACCOMMODATION STAFF ← (bold)

The (advertisement) for two temp accommodation staff will ~~go~~ into the local ~~newspaper~~ paper next Fri evening.

It should be poss to hold interviews two ~~weeks~~ months ✓ later and I plan to reserve the morning of Wed 26 Oct ~~for this purpose~~. I trust this date will not be (inconveneint) for you. [I will ~~send~~ forward the ~~applica~~ applications and any copies of refs to you a week prior to this date ~~for~~ your initial screening.

(for next year)

Copies of the new salary scales are not available at the moment. (however) I am pleased to advise that the induction policy has been (published) and (finalised) and will, therefore, be available for ~~your~~ the new members of yr team.

unit

14

▶ Producing a
business letter

By the end of Unit 14, you should have learnt how to:

▶ recognise the difference between a 'personal business letter' and a
'business letter'

▶ produce a business letter with special marks and enclosure marks

▶ confirm facts by locating information from another document and
including it where indicated

Note: Although Word 97 has an in-built Letter Wizard facility, it is not
entirely suitable for RSA examination purposes.

 Business letter layout ▶

In Unit 10, you learned how to produce a personal business letter on plain A4 paper. In the RSA
Stage I Part 2 Word Processing examination you will be expected to produce a business letter either
by printing it on to a preprinted letterhead form, or by using a template file. You have already learned
how to use both these methods in the previous unit on memoranda, and this unit will allow you further
practice.

▶ *A personal business letter* is the type of formal letter you might write at home to an organisation
or firm referring to matters which are not connected with your work. (Refer back to Unit 10 to
refresh your memory on basic letter layout.)

▶ *A business letter* is written on behalf of an organisation and is printed or typed on the
organisation's own letterhead. An attractive letterhead gives a good impression of the
organisation and contains all relevant details such as telephone and fax numbers. Only the
name and address of the addressee (recipient) of the letter have to be typed because the
sender's details are already printed on the letterhead. The company's letterhead may be stored
as a template file (blueprint) on your computer – you can recall it whenever you need to
complete a company letter.

Special marks and enclosure marks

▶ *Special marks* are designed to draw special attention to instructions such as **CONFIDENTIAL**, **PRIVATE**, **PERSONAL**, **URGENT**, **FOR THE ATTENTION OF** ... on documents and envelopes.

The special mark should be given emphasis such as bold, underline, capitalisation, etc, and placed at the top of the document, usually after the date, with a clear line space above and below it. If a letter includes a special mark, this should also be included on the envelope above the address.

▶ *Enclosure marks* (**Enc** or **Encs**) are used to draw attention to the fact that one or more items should be included with the main document. This alerts the person preparing the mail to check that the item(s) are actually enclosed, and also the person receiving the correspondence to check that the enclosure(s) have actually been included. If an enclosure is found to be missing, appropriate action can then be taken.

The enclosure mark is usually placed at the end of a letter or memo with at least one clear line space above and below it. When using the open style of punctuation the mark Enc or Encs should not have a full stop after it.

 ## Confirming facts

As part of the examination, you will be asked to insert information into a document that can be found in another document. (At work you would be expected to consult paper files, computer databases, etc.) Take notice of the text you are keying in so that you will be able to select the correct piece of information to make your document accurate.

 ## Automatic date insertion

Word will insert the current date in letters and memoranda, as follows:

Keyboard	Mouse/menu
Press: **Alt + Shift + D**	Position the pointer in the correct place for the date to be inserted
	Select: **Insert** from the Menu Bar
	Select: **Date and Time**

The Date and Time dialogue box is displayed on screen (Figure 14.1).

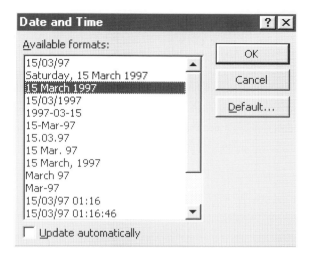

Figure 14.1 Date and Time dialogue box

▶ Word displays a selection of available date formats.
▶ In the UK the third style is usually adopted for letters and memos, ie **15 March 1997**.
▶ Click: The date style you want to insert.
▶ Check: That the **Update automatically** box does *not* have a tick in it – if so, Word would automatically update the date or time whenever you print the document (in some instances, this would be useful)
▶ Click: **OK**

Note: You may select the date style as the default style to save making changes when using the keyboard shortcut: **Alt** + **Shift** + **D**.

 ## Business letter layout: reminders

▶ Block everything at the left-hand margin – do not indent paragraphs or centre items.
▶ Date the letter with today's date – use the automatic date insertion facility to save time.
▶ Use open punctuation – i.e. no punctuation except in the body of the letter.
▶ Leave at least one clear line space between different parts of the letter, and between paragraphs.
▶ If the salutation is formal, eg Dear Sir, use the complimentary close: 'Yours faithfully'.
▶ If the salutation is informal, eg Dear Mr Smith, use the complimentary close: 'Yours sincerely'.
▶ Leave clear lines for the person sending the letter to sign his or her name.
▶ Special marks (e.g. CONFIDENTIAL, PRIVATE, URGENT) should be emphasised with bold, underlining or capitalisation. (The special mark should also be inserted on the envelope.)
▶ If any items are to be included with the letter, type an enclosure mark, Enc(s), at the end of the letter with a clear line space above and below it. Remember, in open punctuation Enc or Encs should *not* be followed by a full stop.

Tip: If Spellchecker stops on the enclosure mark, Enc or Encs, and prompts you to add a full stop, you can simply **Add** the open punctuation version to Spellchecker's dictionary of words so that it does not query it again.

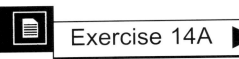

14.1 You have already created a file that you can now use as a letterhead template blueprint. Open the file you saved in Unit 5 as **Letterhead**.

14.2 The 'Better Business Services Ltd' template letter file should now appear on screen ready for you to complete with the rest of the details. Select the **Save As** command from the **File** menu (so that you don't overwrite your letter template file). Use the filename **EX14A**.

14.3 Key in the rest of the letter from the manuscript copy shown as Exercise 14A. (Look back at the letter you completed in Unit 10 to refresh your memory about the parts of a letter.)

Important: Before keying in any additional details, you will need to reset the font to Times New Roman, point size 12. You may also need to alter the margin alignment.

> Our ref: MY/00za9
> Mr B Shields
> 33 Randolph Ave
> BRADFORD
> BD19 3TU
> Dear Mr Shields
>
> <u>Temporary</u>
>
> Position of Accommodations Officer ← (bold + underline)
>
> I am pleased to advise you that you have been shortlisted for the position of A _ O _ (T _).
>
> We intend to hold interviews on the morning of [please insert date from Ex 13B]
>
> Although this is initially a temp post, it is envisaged that the successful candidate will continue in the role, subject to mutually acceptable conditions, when it is made permanent in approx six months' time.
>
> We will begin at 9.30 am with an introductory tour of the co. This will be followed by coffee and an opp to meet other members of the team. (Your) actual interview before the panel is scheduled for 11.15am. Please find enclosed a stamped, addressed envelope for yr reply and a form on which to claim any travel (expences). I would be grateful if you would confirm that you attend on the <u>indicated</u> date.
>
> Yrs scly
> Madeleine Yeats
> PERSONNEL OFFICER
>
> Mark the letter:
> CONFIDENTIAL

14.4 Save your document.. Print your document then check your printout with the key. If you find any errors, retrieve the document and correct any errors.

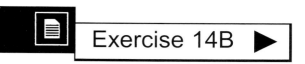

14.5 If you cannot access the printer, complete Exercise 14B in the same way you completed Exercise 14A, using the template file. Otherwise, open the file you saved in Unit 5 as **Letterhead**. Print out a copy. Measure the depth of the preprinted letter heading from the top of the page to the bottom of the heading text and allow for two or three clear line spaces after it. In total, this should be approximately 7.5 cm
(3 in). You are going to print Exercise 14B directly on to this preprinted form in step 14.9. First:

14.6 Close the file **Letterhead**. Starting a new file, key in the following letter, using line spacing as shown.

Our ref: CC/00439
Dr Mr Singh
Order No: RT297 ← (bold + underline)

Send the letter to:
Mr D Singh, 223 Brook Rd,
SHIPLEY, BD18 4TR
and mark the letter:
URGENT

Thank you for yr letter which I recd today.
I was most concerned to note that you had been unable to deliver the consignment of office furniture, ordered by our co, due to delays in yr production. // We have several new secs commencing employment with us next ~~weeks~~ month, for whom the ✓ furniture is required to be in place. (unless) you are able to guarantee a (definate) delivery/within the next 7 days I am afraid we shall have no choice but to (close)our order and(cancel) our acc with you. // I would (apreciate) it if you would contact me within the next 2 days to advise me of yr position.
I would also suggest that you liaise with our Premises Manager, (please insert name of Premises Manager from Exercise 13B), who will make any further arrangements necy. I enclose his bus card for yr reference.
yrs sncly
Jenny Davidson (Ms)
PURCHASING MANAGER

In anticipation of an early delivery,

14.7 Following the instructions given in the previous unit, alter the top margin so that the body of the document does not 'overprint' on top of the preprinted letter heading. Remember, you will probably need to enter a setting of approximately 7.5 cm (3 in) for the top margin in order to allow for several clear line spaces after the letter-heading text.

14.8 Save your document using filename **EX14B**.

14.9 Insert the preprinted letter form (ie the document **Letterhead** which you printed out at step 14.5) correctly into your printer. Print the document: **EX14B** directly on to the letterhead form. Check your printout with the key. If you find any errors, retrieve the document and correct the errors.

14.10 Exit the program if you have finished working or continue straight on to the next unit.

By the end of Unit 15, you should have revised and practised all the techniques and skills needed for the RSA Text Processing Stage I Part 1 Award.

Look at your Progress Review Checklist and at your completed exercises to remind yourself of what you have learned so far and to identify any weaknesses. Then complete the following exercises as revision.

Exercise 15A ▶

15.1   Retrieve your memorandum document template and key in the following text.

From   Cathy Potterton   Training Officer
To   All Unit Supervisors and Section Heads
Ref   CP/TO/2703

The Seminar will be held in Room 201 on Thurs 27 Mar from 9.30 am to approx 12.30 pm. Refreshments will be provided on arrival.

I would like to invite you to attend a half-day one-day Seminar which is to take place at Head Office (please add our address here - from letterhead).

I enclose a copy of the programme for the Seminar which/outlines briefly the content and give the names of the speakers. You will no doubt agree that the issues to be discussed are very important for the health and productivity of our buisness. of the workforce

It is anticipated that all Supervisors and Section Heads will arrange to pass on the info to their teams at briefing sessions as soon as poss. This should take place within three weeks. emphasise sentence

Please take this opp to become informed about co policies, prior to the new legislation coming into force. Complete ✓ the booking form attached, and return to my sec, Lana Knightley.   with your details and sig

double line-spacing please

15.2 Proofread and check your work carefully. Save your work as **EX15A** and print one copy.

Exercise 15B ▶

15.3 Retrieve your letter document and key in the following text

Ref   CP/TO/VID

← ⟨Sales Department⟩

Mega Training PLC
136 Connerton Pl
BRADFIELD
BF2 8LC

Dear Sirs

~~Further to our recent conversation~~ I have received a copy
of yr current cat after discussing our co's training needs
with yr colleagues at the recent Northern Business
Exhibition in Manchester. /we are interested in several of
your products and would welcome the opp to see examples
of yr training materials, including worksheets and
video presentations. I note from the cat that you
recommend a visit by one of your representatives.

✓ ⟨I have completed the necy request card ~~and indicated~~ indicating
our ~~particular~~ special areas of interest, and look forward to
hearing from you. The card is attached to ~~this letter.~~⟩

           must
I ~~need~~ to point out that our training and seminar
accommodation will be ⌊closed⌋ ⌊temporarily⌋ for
refurbishment ⟨from the end of next month.⟩ ← ⟨emphasise⟩
It would therefore be more convenient for us to
~~visit~~ come to yr ~~premises~~ offices during this time.

⟨However, if there is sufficient time to arrange the
presentation in the very near future, our current
facilities would be adequate. ~~Please contact me~~⟩

Yrs ffly

C— P— ⎤ ← ⟨take name and designation from memo⟩
T— O— ⎦

15.4 Proofread and check your work carefully. Save your work as **EX15B** and print one copy.

► Examination Practice 3

By the end of Unit 16, you should have completed a mock examination for the RSA Text Processing Stage I Part 1 Award.

 ## RSA Text Processing Stage I Part I

This examination assesses your ability to produce, from hand-written and type-written draft, a variety of simple documents such as a letter, a memorandum and a short report or article. The award demonstrates that you have acquired elementary skills in word processing (or typewriting). The level of competence relates to NVQ Administration Level 1.

The examination lasts for $1\frac{1}{4}$ hours and you have to complete three documents. Printing is done outside this time.

Examinations are carried out in registered centres and are marked by RSA examiners. The centre will provide A4 plain paper.

Letters must be produced on letterheads (either pre-printed or by use of a template). Memos may be produced on preprinted forms; by keying in entry details, or by use of a template. Remember to insert today's date on letters and memos unless otherwise instructed.

Examination hints

When sitting your examination:

► you may use a manual prepared by the centre or the software manufacturer;
► put your name, centre number and document number on each document;
► check your work very carefully before printing – proofread, spell check; and
► assemble your printouts in the correct order at the end of the examination.

You are now ready to try a mock examinations for Text Processing Stage I Part I. Take care and good luck!

The list of assessment criteria for this examination is long and detailed. To be sure that you have reached the required standard to be entered for an examination, you need to work through several past papers and have these 'marked' by a tutor or assessor who is qualified and experienced in this field.

Results

► If your finished work has 3 faults or fewer, you will be awarded a **distinction**.
► If your finished work has between 4 and 8 faults, you will be awarded a **pass**.

Results are sent to the centre where you sit your examination.

Our ref CP/TO/S103

Ms M Simon
Green Park Consultants Ltd
Green Pk
CHESTER
CH9 7HQ

Dr Ms Simon

I write to confirm our *telephone* conversation earlier today when you kindly agreed to be the keynote speaker at our in-house seminar on *please insert date from Unit 15*. The co places great emphasis on keeping all employees ~~informed~~ up to date with info concerning legislation which *affect* their health and, of course, the org's livelihood.

We are pleased that it is poss for you to pass on yr *such* expertise to us despite being contacted at short notice.

I have forwarded details of the seminar programme to ~~all~~ members of our supervisory staff. Approx 20 places have ~~been~~ reserved for them. The room is equipped with the ~~usual~~ *normal* presentation facilities. Please let me know if you have any special ~~needs~~ requirements.

In addition to ~~programme~~ *Seminar* details, I also enclose a map giving directions from the nearest exit on the M62, and look forward to meeting you at 9.00 am on the above date.

Lunch has been arranged for the main participants and I hope you will join us.

Yrs sncly

Cathy Potterton
Training Officer

Filename: EX16 DOC1

(DOCUMENT 2)   (Memorandum)

From   Cathy Potterton   (put job title here please)

To   Shaheen Zaman   Personal ~~assistant~~ to MD

Ref   CP/TG/S104

We are holding an in-house seminar in the near future and I have asked my new sec, (name from Unit 15), to liaise with you regarding arrangements for (catering) accommodation, equipment, /etc. //As my sec is new to the co, she feels she would like assistance from an experienced member of staff. You were recommended to us as yr work involves dealing with clients, government officials and ~~representatives of~~ foreign visitors.

We would be grateful if you could help with the financial info, practical ~~tasks~~ details, and all the misc tasks necy to the success of such a ~~operation~~ ~~venture~~. ✓

It would help a new colleague by giving her the opp to develop skills and confidence, and would be much appreciated by all concerned.

I did ref my suggestion to ~~Jim~~ Jane Larchwood before writing to you. ~~She~~ She agreed to release you for a few hours next week. ✓ //I hope you enjoy the experience of training – I know this ~~is an~~ area of work is a poss future role you would welcome.

(Filename: EX16DOC2)

(DOCUMENT 3)

WORK-RELATED HEALTH

Company's have a statutory duty to provide a safe workplace for there employees and to protect their physical and mental health. The Health and Safety Acts are designed to ~~legislate for~~ this ✗ happen.
make

double line-spacing

Stress causes both absenteeism and illness. The most stressful jobs are said to be experienced by those in nursing, social work, the police force, and teaching but the highest level of absenteeism is in manual work. Although the use of computers is considered to cause stress in the workplace, it would seem ~~from that this list~~ that it is working with people, perhaps ~~with~~ financial and social constraints, that causes the most stress.
within

Workers in the financial sector show the lowest rates of absenteeism.

However, there are many changes which can be made to help reduce stress. The first step is to understand stress and to recognise where and when it is occurring. It may then be poss to provide a more flexible job structure, alternating high and low stress tasks. Counselling can help some poeple but it may simply be enough for managers and colleagues to listen to problems and respond to them. Some of the larger orgs now offer relaxation and leisure opps to their employees' such as gyms, social events, on-site massage, etc.

Such facilities encourage people to take a break and to do something which will relieve mental tension and the muscular aches and pains which come with it. This may prove a cost-effective and pleasureable way for employers to ~~maintain~~ keep ✓ health and keep the effects of stress to a minimum.

Please emphasise the last paragraph

Filename: EX16 DOC3

unit
17

 Using tables for column work

By the end of Unit 17, you should have learnt how to:

▶ use default tabs
▶ use the Insert Table facility
▶ use the Tables and Borders facility

Using tables for column work ▶

Presenting data in columns is often used within letters, memos and reports to convey information quickly and clearly. Tabulated columns of information are also used for separate tables and accounts. If you align text on screen by pressing the Space Bar it may not line up when you print. It is more accurate to use either Word's table facilities or use the default tab stops which are positioned at regular points on the ruler line. On some keyboards the Tab key is labelled **Tab** and on others shown as $\overset{|\leftarrow}{\rightarrow|}$.

▶ In Word 97 the tab settings are normally defaulted (ie previously set) to every 1.27 cm ($\frac{1}{2}$ in). Each time you press the Tab key you indent the line by 1.27 cm ($\frac{1}{2}$ in). You can often complete a table satisfactorily using the default tabs.
▶ It looks better if you leave approximately equal amounts of space between columns but this is not absolutely necessary.
▶ You should leave at least one clear line after the tabulation work before continuing with any further portions of text (Figure 17.1).

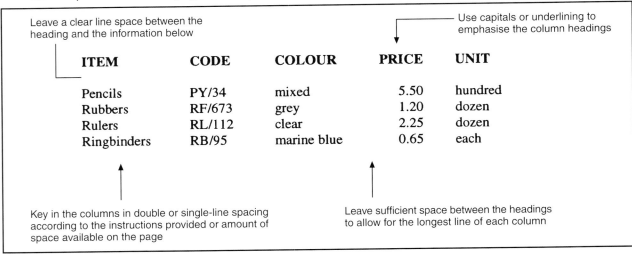

Leave a clear line space between the heading and the information below

Use capitals or underlining to emphasise the column headings

ITEM	CODE	COLOUR	PRICE	UNIT
Pencils	PY/34	mixed	5.50	hundred
Rubbers	RF/673	grey	1.20	dozen
Rulers	RL/112	clear	2.25	dozen
Ringbinders	RB/95	marine blue	0.65	each

Key in the columns in double or single-line spacing according to the instructions provided or amount of space available on the page

Leave sufficient space between the headings to allow for the longest line of each column

Figure 17.1 Table layout

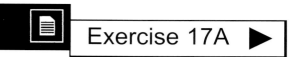

Exercise 17A ▶

17.1 Key in the following text – after typing the month at the beginning of each line, press the Tab key to align the second column at a preset tab stop.

ECONOMIC IMPACT

The following areas must be addressed by the committee members and a full report of intended activities submitted before the end of the month shown below:

MONTH   AREA OF ACTIVITY

June   Regeneration of areas and industries.
July   Business development and overseas investment.
August   Tourism, transport and the environment.
September   Research and development - scientific and agricultural.

17.2 Save and print your document using filename **EX17A**.

Check your printout with the exercise shown above. If you find any errors, retrieve the document and correct.

Creating tables: Insert Table and Tables and Borders facilities ▶

As an alternative to using tabs, you could use the Insert Tables or Tables and Borders facilities to produce table layouts. You will probably need to try out both methods to see which you prefer or find easiest to use.

Insert Table facility
Mouse and Tool Bar method

▶ Position the insertion pointer: Where you want the table to be placed.

▶ Click: The ▦ Insert Table button on the Standard Tool Bar (a drop-down grid of rows and column cells appears on screen).

▶ Select: The number of rows and columns required by moving the mouse pointer across the grid until the bottom of the grid displays the correct layout (eg 4 × 4 table). The grid will increase in size as you drag the mouse. Click the mouse button again.

Menu method

▶ Position the insertion pointer: Where you want the table to be placed.

▶ Select: **Insert Table** from the Table menu.

The Insert Table dialogue box appears on screen (Figure 17.2).

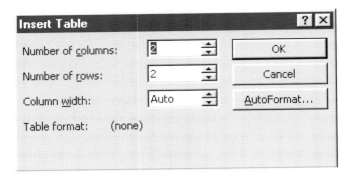

Figure 17.2 Insert Table dialogue box

▶ **Number of columns**	Enter: The required number of vertical columns.
▶ **Number of rows**	Enter: The required number of horizontal rows.
▶ **Column width**	Accept: The default setting (Auto) or select a column width.
▶	Click: **OK**.

To remove borders from a table:

▶ Position the cursor: Anywhere inside the table (after you have set it up).

▶ Select: **Select Table** from the **Table** menu.

▶ Click: The ▼ down arrow on the **Borders** button ⊞ on the Formatting Tool Bar.

▶ Select: The **No Border** button from the drop-down menu. ────────────▶

▶ Click: **OK**.

Tables and Borders facility ⊞
Mouse and tool bar method

▶ Position the insertion pointer: Where you want the table to be placed.

▶ Click: The **Tables and Borders** button on the Standard Tool Bar.

The Tables and Border dialogue box appears on screen (Figure 17.3).

Figure 17.3 Tables and Borders dialogue box

🖊 Use the **Draw Table** tool like a pen to draw your table layout directly on to the screen. Simply click and drag to draw the table outline and the cell divisions inside the table. You can edit the table later to make individual cells any height and width you want.

🖉 Use the **Eraser** tool to remove any cell, row or column partition you don't want, or to merge two adjacent cells vertically or horizontally.

⊞ Use the **Border** tool to set the style of the table's ruled lines. You can choose no lines by selecting the **No Border** button from the drop-down menu. ────────────▲

Note: You will need to select the entire table or the individual cells first to which you wish to apply a border, or no border.

Moving around in a table

Arrow keys	You can move around the table using the appropriate arrow keys.
Tab	Moves right one cell (or inserts a new row when pressed in the last table cell).
Shift + **Tab**	Moves left one cell.
Ctrl + **Tab**	Moves to the next tab stop in the cell.
Alt + **Home** *or* **End**	Moves to the first or last cell in the same row.
Alt + **PgUp** *or* **PgDn**	Moves to the top or bottom cell in the column.
OR	Simply click the mouse pointer in any cell you want to move to!

Selecting items in a table

Using the mouse or menu:

▶ Select: A single cell   Click: The left edge of the cell.

▶ Select: A single row   Click: To the left of the row *or*
Select: **Select Row** from the **Table** menu.

▶ Select: A single column   Click: The column's top gridline or border
or
Select: **Select Column** from the **Table** menu.

▶ Select: Multiple cells, rows or columns   Drag the mouse pointer: Across the cells, rows or columns; *or*
Select: A single cell, row or column, and then hold down the Shift key while you click another cell, row or column.

▶ Select: An entire table   Select: **Select Table** from the **Table** menu.

Using the keyboard:

▶ Select: The next cell's contents	Press: **Tab**.
▶ Select: The preceding cell's contents	Press: **Shift** + **Tab**.
▶ Extend a selection to adjacent cells	Hold down: **Shift** *and* **press an arrow key repeatedly**.
▶ Select: A column(s)	Click: In the column's top or bottom cell. Hold down: **Shift** and press: The ↑ Up arrow or the ↓ Down arrow key repeatedly.
▶ Extend a selection (or block)	Press: **CTRL** + **Shift** + **F8**, then use the arrow keys to extend in the required direction; Press **Esc** to cancel selection mode.
▶ Reduce the selection size	Press: **Shift** + **F8**.
▶ Select: An entire table	Press: **ALT** + **5** on the numeric keypad (with Num Lock off).

Changing column width in a table

Mouse	**Menu**
▶ Select: The column(s) to be changed. ▶ Point to: The column-dividing line and Press: The left mouse button (keep holding it down – the pointer changes to a ◀╫▶double-headed arrow).	▶ Click: In the column(s) to be changed. ▶ Select: **Table**, **Cell Height** and **Width**, **Column**. ▶ *Either*

▶ Drag: The column dividing line to the left or right to increase or decrease the column width as appropriate.

▶ Release: The mouse button.

1 Enter: The appropriate measurement in the **Width of Column** box *or*

2 Select: **AutoFit** to resize the columns automatically so the width fits the content.

▶ Click: **OK**.

Note: You can also specify the amount of space between columns if required.)

To make several columns or cells exactly the same width:

▶ Select: The columns or cells.

▶ Select: **Distribute Columns Evenly** from the **Table** menu *or*

▶ Click: The ▦ button in the **Tables and Borders** dialogue box.

Changing row height in a table

Mouse

▶ Select: The row(s) to be changed.

▶ In 🔲 Page Layout View: Point to the row marker (dividing line) on the vertical ruler and hold the left mouse button down:

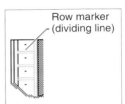

The pointer changes to a vertical double-headed arrow ↕.

▶ Drag: The row-dividing line up or down to increase or decrease the row height as appropriate.

▶ Release: The mouse button.

Menu

▶ Click: The row(s) to be changed.

▶ Select: **Table**, **Cell Height and Width**, **Row**.

▶ Enter: The appropriate measurement in the **Height of Rows** and **At** boxes.

▶ Click: **OK**.

(*Note*: You can also specify any row alignment and/or indent if required.)

To make several rows or cells exactly the same height:

▶ Select: The rows or cells.

▶ Select: **Distribute Rows Evenly** from the **Table** menu *or*

▶ Click: The ▤ button in the **Tables and Borders** dialogue box.

Inserting columns and rows in a table

Position the insertion pointer at the place where you wish to insert another column or row:

▶ Select: **Select Row** *or* **Select Column** from the **Table** menu.

▶ Select: **Insert Rows** or **Insert Columns** from the **Table** menu.

▶ *or* Press: The right mouse button and Select: **Insert Rows/Insert Columns**

▶ *or* with the insertion pointer in the table, Click: The ⤵ **Insert Rows** button on the Standard Tool Bar.

Note: Sometimes when you insert a column the last one goes outside the margin. You will have to change to Normal View to pick up the right border and pull it back.

Deleting columns and rows in a table

Position the insertion pointer at the place where you wish to make the deletion:

▶ Select: **Select Row** *or* **Select Column** from the **Table** menu.

▶ Select: **Delete Rows/Delete Columns** from the **Table** menu *or*

▶ Select: **Table**, **Delete Cells**, **Delete entire column** or **Delete entire row**.

▶ *or* Press: The right mouse button and Select: **Delete Rows**

▶ *or* Select: The column to be deleted; Press: The right mouse button and Select: **Delete Columns**.

Aligning text or data in a column or row

You can align the text or data in each individual column or row in the normal way by selecting one of the Alignment buttons on the Formatting Tool Bar

▶ Select: The column(s) or row(s) you want to set the alignment for.

▶ Click: On the appropriate alignment button on the Formatting Tool Bar.

Removing borders/lines from a table

▶ Click: The insertion pointer anywhere inside the table.

▶ Select: **Select Table** from the **Table** menu.

▶ Click: The down arrow on the **Borders** button ▢ on the Formatting Tool Bar.

▶ Select: ▨ **No Borders** option from the drop-down menu.

Exercise 17B: practice exercise ▶

17.3 Starting a new document, use the Insert Table facility to create a table with 4 rows and 4 columns. Practise:

▶ moving around the table

▶ changing the column width and row height

▶ inserting a row and inserting a column

▶ deleting a row and deleting a column

▶ entering data in the table

▶ aligning the data in each column to the left, right and centre

▶ removing borders/lines from the table.

17.4 Repeat the above using the ▦ Tables and Borders facility.

17.5 Close the file without saving so that you are ready to start the next exercise with a clear screen.

17.6 Use the **Insert Table** or **Table and Borders** facilities to reproduce the following piece of work. Ensure that you have selected right alignment for the third and fourth columns.

Maynard's Mad March Specials

ITEM	REF NO	OLD PRICE	NEW PRICE
Salad servers	SS356	£3.50	£2.99
Cruet set	CS775	£2.99	£2.50
Lace tablecloth	LT112	£14.99	£12.99

17.7 Press ↵ (return/enter) several times to leave a gap before the next piece of work. Align the text in the columns as shown.

NEW EVENING COURSES

COURSE	STAGE	ROOM NO	TUTOR
Word processing	Stage1 part 1	B60	Martin Thompson
Word processing	Stage 1 part 2	B22	Celia Brown
Typewriting	Stage 3 part 1	A2	Mavis Graney
Shorthand	Stage 2	A34	Fiona Dearing

17.8 Press ↵ (return/enter) several times to leave a gap before the next piece of work. Align the text in the columns as shown.

SCHOOL RACE DAY

Race	Start time	Finish time	Arena
Sack race	1430 hours	1445 hours	B
Egg and spoon	1500 hours	1515 hours	A
Three legged	1530 hours	1545 hours	C
Relay	1600 hours	1630 hours	B

17.9 Save and print your document using filename **EX17C**. Check your printout with the exercises shown above. If you find any errors, correct them and print again if necessary.

17.10 Exit the program if you have finished working or continue straight on to the next unit.

► Page numbering, indenting text and changing document line length

By the end of Unit 18, you should have learnt how to:

► insert page breaks and number continuation sheets
► indent blocks of text or paragraphs
► change the line length for the whole document

Pagination for continuation sheets ►

When you are keying in a long document of several pages, Word automatically inserts 'soft' page breaks for you. In Normal View mode, a page break is shown by a horizontal dotted line on screen with the words **Page Break** in the centre of the line. The printer will start a new page at this point. However, you may need to insert new page breaks yourself in a specific place – these are often called 'hard' page breaks. Page breaks should be inserted in sensible places within a document so that it is easy to read. When paginating (inserting page breaks):

✗ the complimentary close of a letter (Yours …) should never be the *only* text on the last page;
✗ you should not divide a word between one page and the next;
✗ you should not leave only the first line of a paragraph at the bottom of a page (a 'widow'); and
✗ you should not carry forward only the last line of a paragraph on to the next page (an 'orphan').

Widow/orphan control

Word allows you to avoid widows and orphans automatically. Check that Word is defaulted to do this:

Select: **Format, Paragraph, Line and Page Breaks**.

Check: That the widow/orphan box is ticked.
All other boxes should be blank.

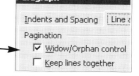

Insert a new page break
Keyboard   Mouse and menu

Position insertion pointer: Where you want to insert the page break:

Press: **Ctrl + ↵** (return)   Select: **Insert, Break, Page break, OK**.

It is customary to number the pages of a multi-page document so that readers can follow the page sequence more easily. Word has a page numbering command that allows you to set the page numbers once so that page numbers will then appear automatically on all pages of the document.

In some instances you may not want the page number to appear on page one, e.g. the first page of a multi-page letter is not usually numbered. You can tell Word not to show the number on the first page where appropriate. However, RSA have stated that numbering the first page will not actually incur any penalties.

Insert page numbers
Mouse and menu

Select: **Page Numbers** from the **Insert** menu.

The Page Numbers dialogue box is displayed on screen (Figure 18.1).

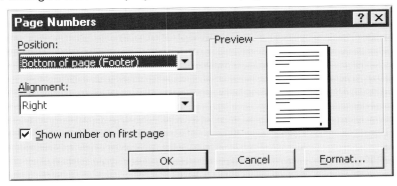

Figure 18.1   Page Numbers dialogue box

Page numbering offers choice of **Position, Alignment, Show number on first page**

The **Preview** box allows you to see the position of the page number.

Note: Page numbers show on screen in Page Layout View and Print Preview only.

Select from the Page Numbers dialogue box as appropriate:

Button	Action
Position	Select position on page *vertically* – **Bottom** (footer) or **Top** (header).
Alignment	Select position on page *horizontally* – **Left**, **Right** or **Centre** (**Inside** and **Outside** are used with binding margins).
Show number on first page	Remove ✔ if you don't want a number to appear on the first page (eg on a multi-page letter).
Preview	Displays page number in position chosen.
Format	Allows a different format of page number to be selected, (eg letter).
Page numbering	Allows you to decide on the page numbering sequence.

Indent: 'wrap around' or temporary indent feature ▶

In Unit 3 you practised changing the left and right margins to inset the text to a different line length. Another method of indenting blocks of text, or paragraphs, is to use Word's Indent function.

You should not confuse paragraph indentation with setting left and right margins (see Figure 18.2). The margins set the overall width of the main text and the amount of space between the main text and the edges of the page. 'Indenting' moves the text in or out from the margins. If you are asked to leave a specified amount of horizontal space at any point in a task, you may choose to use either the Indent function or alter the margin settings as appropriate.

When you operate the Indent function, the insertion pointer moves to the first preset tab stop (usually defaulted to 1.3 cm or $\frac{1}{2}$ in from the left margin). As you carry on keying in, the text will 'wrap around' the indent point until you operate the command to go back to the original left margin.

In Word, you can choose to indent paragraphs in different ways. You can choose to indent the text from both the left margin and right margins or from the left margin only.

It is often more convenient to use the Indent function to indent a single paragraph, rather than changing the margins.

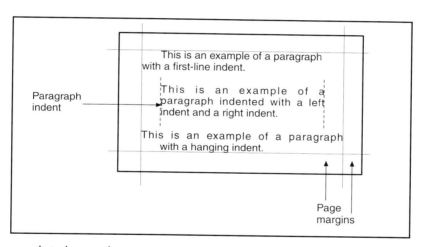

Figure 18.2 Paragraph indent and page margins

Indenting a portion of text e.g. paragraph(s)
Using the keyboard

Indent: To the next tab stop	Press: **Ctrl + M**
Indent: To the previous tab stop	Press: **Ctrl + Shift + M**
Inden: As a hanging paragraph	Press: **Ctrl + T** (*or* Press: **Tab** key)
Remove indent and return to standard margins	Press: **Ctrl + Q**

Using the Formatting Tool Bar

Indent: To the next tab stop	Click: The **Increase Indent** button
Indent: To the previous tab stop	Click: The **Decrease Indent** button

Using the ruler

▶ Select: **Ruler** from the **View** menu to display the horizontal ruler on screen (unless it is already visible) and ensure you are in **Page Layout View**.

▶ Select: The paragraph(s) you want to indent.

▶ Drag: The indent markers to the required position on the horizontal ruler.

To set **Right Indent**:	Drag: △		To set **First Line Indent**:	Drag: ▽
To set **Left Indent**:	Drag: ⬗		To set **Hanging Indent**:	Drag: ⬠

To set a **Negative** indent, i.e. scroll into the left margin:

Hold down: **Shift**; Click on the left first-line indent marker and drag to required position.

As you drag the margin indent, press and hold down the **Alt** key to see the exact measurement on the ruler.

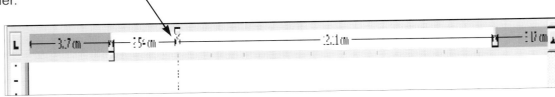

Figure 18.3 Ruler with measurements showing

This method lets you view measurements on screen. By holding down the **Alt** key as you click the mouse pointer on the left or right margin boundary or indent, you will be able to see the measurements of the margins, indents and typing line length displayed across the horizontal ruler.

Using the menu

▶ Select: **Ruler** from the **View** menu to display the horizontal ruler on screen (unless it is already visible) and ensure you are in **Page Layout View**.

▶ Select: The paragraph(s) you want to indent.

▶ From the **Format** menu, Select: **Paragraph**, **Indents and Spacing**.

The Indents and Spacing dialogue box is displayed on screen (Figure 18.4).

▶ Select: The paragraph alignment from the **Alignment** drop-down box.

▶ Select or key in: The **Left** and **Right** indent measurements required in the **Indentation** boxes.

▶ Select: **First Line** or **Hanging** indents (or none) from the list in the **Special** drop-down box.

▶ Select: An alternative measurement for the first-line or hanging indent from the **By** drop-down box if the default one is not appropriate.

▶ Click: **OK**.

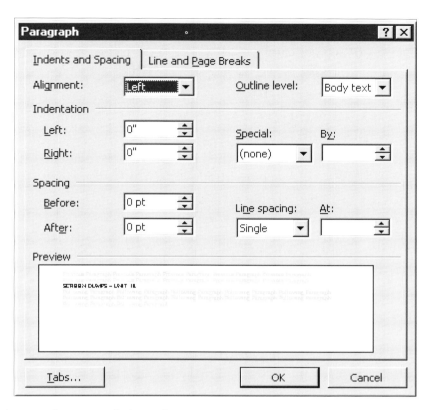

Figure 18.4 Indents and Spacing dialogue box

  Changing the typing length ▶

You may be asked to change the 'typing line length' (or typing line) of a document to a fixed number of characters. This is achieved by *insetting the margins* or *indenting* using the indent function. (It is not always possible in word processing to be completely accurate in this respect and examiners should be aware of this and be lenient in their marking of this feature.)

The width of an A4 page is 21 cm (8 $\frac{1}{4}$ in). The typing line length is the difference between the page width and the two margin measurements.

For example, if the left and right margins are both set by default to 2.54 cm (1 in):

width of A4 page   = 21.00 cm (8.25 in)
minus left margin   –   2.54 cm (1.00 in)
minus right margin –   2.54 cm (1.00 in)

typing line length = 15.92 cm (6.25 in)

(See Figure 18.5.)

To increase or decrease the typing line length, you must adjust the margin settings.

As shown in Figure 18.5, if you were asked to set a typing line length of 11.5 cm (4.5 in) you would need to increase both the left and right margins to 4.75 cm (1.88/1.87 in).

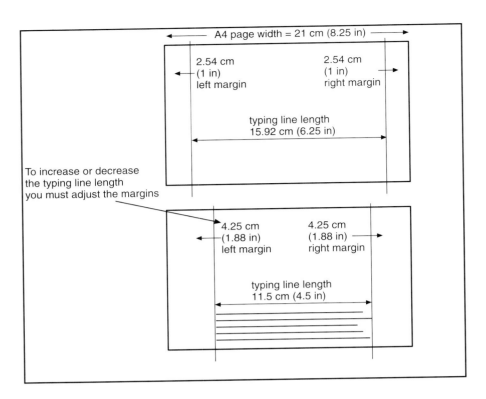

Figure 18.5 Changing the typing line length

To change the typing line length for the whole document

You can use either of the methods detailed below to change the margins before or after keying in the document text:

1   You could select **Page Setup** from the **File** menu to change the margins – refer back to the instructions shown earlier in Unit 3. You will first need to calculate what the new margin settings will need to be in order to determine the appropriate typing line length (as shown above).

2   You could use the mouse and ruler method so that you can see the margin markers move on screen – refer back to the instructions shown earlier in Unit 3. Remember to ensure that you are in **Page Layout View**. Press and hold down the **Alt** key as you point to the margin boundary markers on the horizontal ruler. This will enable you to view the exact typing line length measurement on the document screen (Figure 18.6).

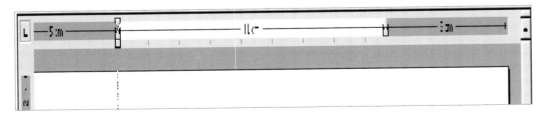

Figure 18.6 Typing line length

You may even wish to use a combination of the two methods, ie change the left and right margins using the Page Setup method, then check the typing line length on the horizontal ruler using the Alt key facility.

To change the typing line length for part of a document

Follow the instructions given earlier in this unit, 'Indenting a portion of text e.g. paragraph(s)'.

Note: In RSA examinations, it is not necessary for left and right margins to be equal, although this does give a balanced appearance to a document. It is acceptable to change the typing line length by changing *only* the left or right margin. However, in practice, you will be governed by certain things: eg house style, author's preference, whether the document is to be inserted into a binder etc.

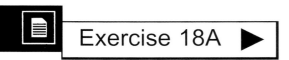

18.1 Retrieve the file you saved from Unit 4: **EX4C**. Change the line spacing for the whole document to double-line spacing and underline the main heading. Ensure the document has a ragged right margin throughout.

18.2 Change the typing line length of the whole document to **7.6 cm** (**3 in**). Using the Indent function, indent the second paragraph by a further **2.54 cm** (**1 in**) at the left margin.

18.3 Number the continuation page only at bottom right of the page (ie no page numbering on first page). Use the Print Preview facility to check that your work is displayed correctly before printing.

18.4 Save and print your document using filename **EX18A**. Check your printout with the key. If your layout does not match, reread the information and amend.

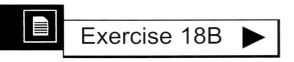

18.5 Retrieve the file you saved from Unit 6: **EX6B**. Change the line spacing for the whole document to double-line spacing, apart from the last paragraph which should remain in single-line spacing. Ensure the document has a justified right margin throughout.

18.6 Change the typing line length of the whole document to **8.9 cm** (**3.5 in**). Using the Indent function:

▶ indent the second and fourth paragraphs by a further **2.54 cm** (**1 in**) at left margin only; and
▶ indent the last paragraph by a further **1.27 cm** ($\frac{1}{2}$ **in**) at left and right margins.

18.7 Number the continuation page only at bottom centre of the page. Insert a page break for the second page just before the fourth paragraph of the document.

18.8 Save and print your document using filename **EX18B**. Check your printout with the key. If your layout does not match, reread the information and amend.

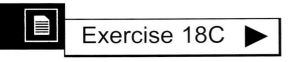

18.9 Starting a new file, key in the following exercise:

THE BENEFITS OF BRANDING

<u>**What is a brand?**</u>

difference

The dictionary defines the ~~contrast~~ between a product and a brand as follows:

PRODUCT: *result of process of manufacture*
BRAND: *trademark, particular quality (of goods)*

The term 'product' applies to an undifferentiated range of commodities (or services). For example, milk, eggs and cheese are known as dairy products. On the other hand, 'Goldenlay' is a unique, identifiable brand of eggs; 'Kraft' is a unique, identifiable brand of cheese. Brands have a unique name and often their own logo, design and packaging. They may be classified as:

<u>Brand types</u>   <u>Examples</u>

Company brands   Morphy Richards, Dorlux, Panasonic
House brands   Kayes, Burlington, Janet Frazer
                             (all belong to the same catalogue firm)

Umbrella brands   Polyfilla, Polycell, Easicell
Individual brands   Kellogg's Cornflakes, Big Mac
Distributors brands Marks & Spencer
                             (distribute St Michael brands)

<u>**Advantages of developing a brand**</u>

Giving products unique 'personalities' distinguishes them from their competitors. Getting the consumer to recognise benefits and advantages associated with a particular brand represents a considerable long-term investment for the organisation. An established reputation requires relatively less expenditure than competitors in order to maintain sales. Superior profitability offers more liberal choices in decision-making for future investments in quality improvement of further marketing expenditure. Company take-overs where strong brands exist demonstrate much higher prices being paid.

<u>**Customer perceptions and brand functions**</u>

For a brand to be successful, its identity must be immediately clear. Also, the brand should reflect a summary of information and associations which is triggered off in the consumer's memory. Consumers need to feel secure in their purchase and that the familiar brand guarantees added value such as better quality or better value for money. Building and maintaining the brand is a central function of marketing and ~~critical~~ essential to the ✓ profitability of the organisation.

18.10 Save and print your document, using the filename **EX18C**. Check your document against the printout check in the key. If you find any errors, correct them and print again if necessary.

18.11 Exit the program if you have finished working or continue straight on to the next unit.

► Consolidation 2

By the end of Unit 19 you should have revised and practised all the techniques and skills needed for the RSA Text Processing Stage I Part 2 Award.

Look at your Progress Review Checklist and at your completed exercises to remind yourself of what you have learned so far and to identlfy your weaknesses. Then complete the following exercises as revision.

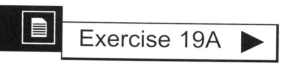

Exercise 19A ►

Recall the document stored under filename **EX18C**. Amend as shown. Use a ragged right margin (except where indicated). Number continuation sheets only at bottom centre. Make sure your name is positioned at the top of each piece of work before saving.

Save and print a copy of your file – use the filename **EX19A**.

[re-position the page break for page 2 in a sensible place]

THE BENEFITS OF BRANDING [centre]

What is a brand? [CAPS]

The dictionary defines the difference between a product and a brand ~~as follows~~ [in the following way]:

[indent this section by 13 mm (½ in) from left margin]

PRODUCT: ***result of process of manufacture***
BRAND: ***trademark, particular quality (of goods)***

The term 'product' ~~applies to~~ [signifies] an undifferentiated range of commodities (or services). For example, milk, cheese and eggs are ~~known~~ [classed] as dairy products. On the other hand, 'Goldenlay' is a unique, identifiable brand of eggs; 'Kraft' is a unique, identifiable brand of cheese.

Brands have a unique name and often their own logo, design and packaging. They may be classified as:

[• start this section at left margin • make Ref the middle column, eg Brand types Ref Examples]

Ref	Brand types	Examples
A)	Company ~~brands~~	Morphy Richards, Dorlux, Panasonic
B)	House ~~brands~~	Kayes, Burlington, Janet Frazer ~~*(all belong to the same catalogue firm)*~~
C)	Umbrella ~~brands~~	Polyfilla, Polycell, Easicell
D)	Individual ~~brands~~	Kellogg's Cornflakes, Big Mac
E)	Distributors ~~brands~~	Marks & Spencer ~~*(distribute St Michael brands)*~~

Advantages of developing a brand (CAPS)

Giving products unique 'personalities' distinguishes them from their competitors. Getting the consumer to recognise benefits and advantages associated with a particular brand represents a considerable long-term investment for the organisation.

An established reputation requires relatively less expenditure than competitors in order to maintain sales. Superior profitability offers more liberal choices in decision-making for future investments in quality improvement of further marketing expenditure. Company take-overs where strong brands exist demonstrate much higher prices being paid.

Customer perceptions and brand functions ← (CAPS)

For a brand to be successful, its identity must be immediately clear. Also,

the brand should reflect a summary of information and associations which is

triggered off in the consumer's memory. [Consumers need to feel secure in

their purchase and that the familiar brand guarantees added value such as

better quality or better value for money. Through continual marketing activity and brand recognition, a more rapid means of memory interrogation minimises information search and evaluation, thereby reducing the effort needed to make the purchase.

Building and maintaining the brand is a central function of marketing and

critical to the profitability of the organisation.

Some organisations have been so successful in marketing their products that the brand name has become a synonym for the product. For example 'Flymo' is often used to mean lawn mower.

Insert at the point marked ✳ and inset by 2.54 cm (1 in) at left margin

Operator
a) add text emphasis to all words underlined with a wavy line ∿∿∿
b) change 'consumer' to 'customer' throughout document
c) use single-line spacing throughout the document and a typing line length of 14 cm (5½ in).

unit

20 ▶ Examination Practice 4

By the end of Unit 20, you should have completed a mock examination for the RSA Text Processing Stage I Part 2 Award.

RSA Word Processing Stage I Part 2 ▶

This examination assesses your ability to produce, from hand-written and type-written draft, a variety of simple documents such as a notice, an article and a simple table. The award demonstrates that you have acquired elementary skills in word processing. The level of competence relates to NVQ Administration Level 1.

The examination lasts for $1\frac{1}{2}$ hours and you have to complete three documents. Printing is done outside this time.

Examinations are carried out in registered centres and are marked by RSA examiners. The centre will provide A4 plain paper.

Examination hints

When sitting your examination:

▶ you may use a manual prepared by the centre or the software manufacturer;
▶ put your name, centre number and document number on each document;
▶ check your work very carefully before printing – proofread, spell check; and
▶ assemble your printouts in the correct order at the end of the examination.

You are now ready to try a mock examination for Word Processing Stage I Part 2. Take care and good luck!

The list of assessment criteria for this examination is long and detailed. To be sure that you have reached the required standard to be entered for an examination, you need to work through several past papers and have these 'marked' by a tutor or assessor who is qualified and experienced in this field.

Results

▶ If your finished work has three faults or fewer, you will be awarded a *distinction*.
▶ If your finished work has between four and seven faults, you will be awarded a *pass*.

Results are sent to the centre where you sit your examination.

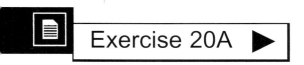

Recall the document stored under filename **EX6D**. Amend as shown. Adjust the line length to 11.5 cm ($4\frac{1}{2}$ in). Format the document to single-line spacing throughout (except where indicated) and use a ragged right margin. Number continuation sheets. Make sure your name is positioned at the top of each piece of work before saving.

Save and print a copy of your file – use the filename: **EX20A**.

---

its origins

HISTORY OF ADVERTISING AND MEDIA EXPANSION

Advertising has been around for many centuries, and can be traced back to the days of ancient Greece, where historians found the first clear evidence of advertising being used for commercial purposes.

The first signs of media expansion developed through printing in the

latter
~~second~~ half of the 15th century which offered a whole new dimension. *It was several centuries later, however, towards* ~~However, it was not until~~ the end of the Industrial Revolution (late 18th century) that advertising began to [really] establish itself. By the 20th century a massive media expansion was making its impact on society.

\#   *move to point marked ✱*

During the 19th century, a number of factors combined to stimulate the expansion of advertising in Britain. One of the most important was the development of large industrial companies putting the mass output theories of Adam Smith into practice, and using economies of scale ~~(buying raw materials in bulk at a cheaper price)~~ to turn out massive quantities of goods at a lower unit price. *inset this paragraph by 2.54 cm (1") from left margin and put in double line spacing*

In order to maintain the output of such large quantities of food, soap, clothing and other items, these firms needed to develop mass consumption as well as mass output. *If companies were to buy in* ~~bulk~~ *bulk at cheaper prices, they also needed to sell in bulk to sustain adequate profit margins.*

(Start a new page here)

Introduction of the Newspaper ◄── (bold)

most effective way of achieving ~~this~~

The ~~best way of doing~~ this, since they could not afford to employ enough salesmen to sell to the whole population in person, was by advertising.

This led to the development of the most important single medium for the communication of ideas, opinions, knowledge and advertisements - the newspaper. [The newspaper was the first recognised modern mass medium. ✳

Newspapers were not a 19th century invention, although their output, format and readerships changed considerably during that period as they became industrialised.

The Industrial Revolution gave newspapers the kick-start needed to mature from a form of media that was only ~~reports~~ reporting on local stories.

Operator
Replace the word 'output' with 'production' throughout the document

inset this paragraph by 1.27 cm (½") from left and right margins and put in double line spacing

As Industry replaced traditional craftsmanship with machine-based mass output, people moved from rural areas into urban areas for the large numbers of jobs that became available. Towns and cities increased in their house numbers and population size. The new jobs and new houses also needed to be advertised as well as the new products.

insert this paragraph at the point marked #

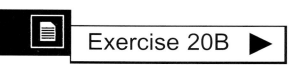
Recall the document stored under filename **EX5E**. Amend as shown. Use a justified right margin (except where indicated). Save and print a copy of your file – use the filename **EX20B**.

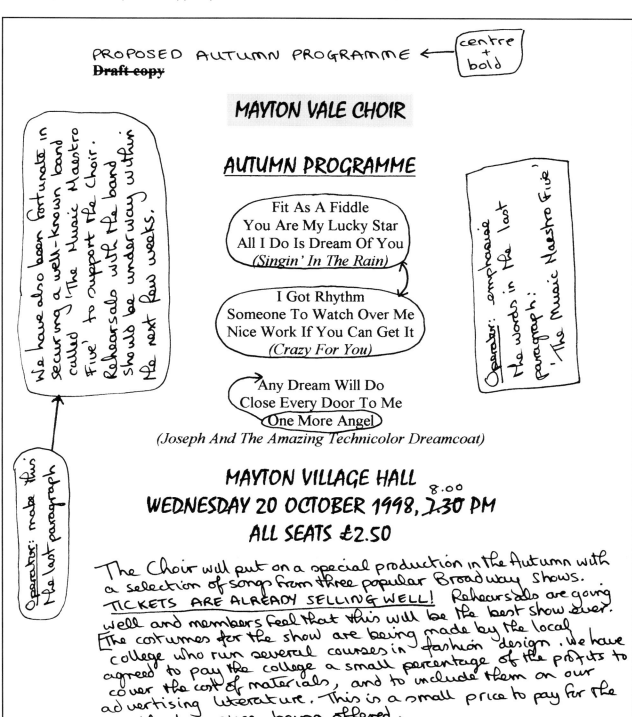

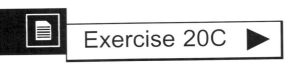

Recall the document stored under filename **EX17A**. Amend as shown. Use a justified right margin. Save and print a copy of your file – use the filename **EX20C**.

ECONOMIC IMPACT REPORT ← (centre)

The following areas must be addressed by the committee members and a full report of intended activities submitted before the end of the month shown below:

Operator: please align the MONTH END column to the right and expand all the abbreviated month names in full

MONTH	AREA OF ACTIVITY
June	Regeneration of areas and industries.
July	Business development and overseas investment.
August	Tourism, transport and the environment.
September	Research and development - scientific and agricultural.

In order to obtain (timely) and (comprehensive) information needed for the final report, it is suggested that committee members undertake the areas of responsibility detailed below:

NAME	MONTH END	SPECIALISM
Wayne Anderson	July	Enterprise
Pauline Bretton	June	Transport Logistics
Lavinia de Courcy	June	Urban Regeneration
Margaret Haugh	August	Environmental Studies
Matthew Hart	June	Business Development
Vera Kadinsky	June	International Trade
Samantha Prescott	September	Research Studies
Mohammed Saleed	June	Industrial Development
Mark Schmitt	Sep	Agriculture
Joanne Turner	Aug	Travel and Tourism
Tim Wetherspoon	Sep	Chemical Plant
Lewis Young	Aug	Green Studies

DO NOT RULE

Members should ensure that they are able to access word-processing facilities in order to provide their document file on disk as well as hard copy. Marjorie Faulkes, Sec to the Chairman, will collate each individual report into a final document ready for the next Planning Group meeting.

Please modify the layout by keying in the MONTH END column after the SPECIALISM column, eg

NAME	SPECIALISM	MONTH END
Wayne Anderson	Enterprise	July

Progress review checklist

Unit	Topic	Date completed	Comments
▶ 1	Load Word 97 for Windows program		
	Open a new document/file		
	Key in text		
	Move cursor around document		
	Edit text (delete/insert)		
	Split/join paragraphs		
	Save work to correct disk drive/directory		
	Print a document		
	Close a file		
	Exit Word 97 for Windows program		
▶ 2	Open an existing file		
	Select a block of text		
	Delete/cut a block of text		
	Restore deleted text		
	Move a block of text		
	Copy a block of text		
▶ 3	Ragged right margin		
	Justified right margin		
	Units of measurement		
	Change margins		
	Line spacing – double and single		
	Print Preview document before printing		
▶ 4	AutoCorrect and AutoFormat		
	Spelling and grammar check		
	Find (search) and replace text		
▶ 5	Emphasise text – bold, underline, italic		
	Highlight/shade text		
	Centre text		
	Change font style		
	Change font size		
▶ 6	Examination Practice 1 (CLAIT)		
▶ 7	Use text correction signs		
	Common abbreviations		
	Spelling in context		
	Typographical errors		
▶ 8	Unfamiliar/foreign words		
	Errors of agreement		
	Grammar check		

Unit	Topic	Date completed	Comments
▶ 9	Working from manuscript copy		
	Reading hand-writing		
	Producing a notice from hand-written text		
▶ 10	Personal business letter layout		
	Fully blocked style		
	Open punctuation		
	Insert a new page break		
▶ 11	Examination Practice 2		
	(RSA Initial Text Processing award)		
▶ 12	Basic correction signs		
	Additional abbreviations		
	Spelling in context		
	Rearranging text		
▶ 13	Memorandum		
	Preprinted forms and templates		
	Altering the document top margin		
	Use of keyboard Tab key		
▶ 14	Business letter layout		
	Special marks and enclosure marks		
	Confirming facts		
	Automatic date insertion		
▶ 15	Consolidation Practice 1		
▶ 16	Examination Practice 3		
	(RSA Text Processing Stage I Part 1)		
▶ 17	Using tables for column work		
	Insert Tables facility		
	Tables and Borders facility		
	Moving around in a table		
	Selecting items in a table		
	Changing column width in a table		
	Changing row height in a table		
	Inserting columns and rows in a table		
	Deleting columns and rows in a table		
	Aligning text or data in a column or row		
	Removing borders/lines from the table		
▶ 18	Text formatting		
	Widow/orphan control		
	Page numbering for continuation sheets		
	Indent function		
	Change the typing line length		
▶ 19	Consolidation Practice 2		
▶ 20	Examination Practice 4		
	(RSA Word Processing Stage I Part 2)		

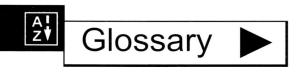

Glossary ▶

Action	Keyboard	Mouse	Menu
Alignment of text	*See*: Ragged right margins. Centre text, Justified right margin		
Allocate clear lines	Press: ↵ once for each line required, plus one		
AutoCorrect			**Tools, AutoCorrect**
AutoFormat	Press: **Alt + Ctrl + K**		**Format, AutoFormat**
Blocked capitals	Press: **Caps Lock** key		
Bold text	Press: **Ctrl + B**	Click: **B** on the Formatting Tool Bar	**Format, Font**
Borders		Click: 🔲 on the Formatting Tool Bar	**Format, Borders and Shading, Borders**
Capitalise letters	Press: **Ctrl + Shift + A**		**Format, Change Case, Uppercase**
Case of letters (to change)	Press: **Shift + F3**		**Format, Change Case**
Centre text	Press: **Ctrl + E**	Click: ☰ on the Formatting Tool Bar	**Format, Paragraph, Indents and Spacing, Alignment, Centred**
Close a file (clear screen)	Press: **Ctrl + W**		**File, Close**
Copy a block of text Highlight text to be copied	Press: **Ctrl + C**	Click: 📋 on the Standard Tool Bar *or* Press: Right mouse button and select: **Copy**	**Edit, Copy**
Position cursor where text is to be copied to	Press: **Ctrl + V**	Click: 📋 on the Standard Tool Bar *or* Press: Right mouse button and Select: **Paste**	**Edit, Paste**
Cursor movement Move cursor to required position	Use arrow keys: → ↑ ← ↓	Click: The left mouse button in required position	
Move to top of document	Press: **Ctrl + Home**		
Move to end of document	Press: **Ctrl + End**		
Move left word by word	Press: **Ctrl + ←**		
Move right word by word	Press: **Ctrl + →**		
Move to end of line	Press: **End**		
Move to start of line	Press: **Home**		
Move to top/bottom of paragraph	Press: **Ctrl + ↑** *or* **Ctrl + ↓**		
Move up/down one screen	Press: **PgUp** *or* **PgDn**		
Cut text	*See* Delete/cut a block of text		
Date insertion	Press: **Alt + Shift + D**		**Insert, Date and Time**
Delete/cut a block of text	Select: Text to be deleted	Select: Text to be deleted/cut:	Select: Text to be deleted/cut:
	Press: ← (**Del**) *or* Select: Text to be deleted; Press **Ctrl + X**	Click: ✂ on the Formatting Tool Bar	Select: **Edit, Cut** *or* Press: Right mouse button; select: **Cut**
Delete/cut a character	Move cursor to correct character; Press: **Del** *or* Move cursor to right of incorrect character; Press:← (**Del**)		
Delete/cut a word	Select: To end of word	Select: Word to be deleted/cut:	Select: Word to be deleted/cut:
	Press: ← (**Del**) *or* Select: Word to be deleted: Press: **Ctrl + X**	Click: ✂ on the Formatting Tool Bar	Select: **Edit, Cut** *or* Press: Right mouse button; select: **Cut**

Action	Keyboard	Mouse	Menu
Exit the program	Press: **Alt + F4**	Click: Control button at right of Title Bar	**File, Exit**
Find text	Press: **Ctrl + F**		**File, Find**
Font size	Press: **Ctrl + Shift + P** Choose: Desired size	Click: 10 ▾ on the Formatting Tool Bar Choose: Desired size	**Format, Font** Choose: Desired size
Next larger point size Next smaller point size	Press: **Ctrl +]** Press: **Ctrl + [**		
Font typeface style	Press: **Ctrl + Shift + F** Choose: Desired font	Click: Times on the Formatting Tool Bar Choose: Desired font	**Format, Font** Choose: Desired font
Go to (a specified page)	Press: **Ctrl + G** or **F5**		**Edit, Go To …**
Grammar tool	Press: **F7**	Click: ABC✓ on the Standard Tool Bar	**Tools, Spelling and Grammar**
Help function and Office Assistant	Press: **F1** (for Contents) Press: **Shift + F1** (for **What's This?** – context-sensitive help)	Click: [?] on the Formatting Tool Bar for the **Office Assistant**	**Help**
Highlight/shade text		Click: ✎ on the Formatting Tool Bar	**Format, Borders and Shading, Shading**
Indent function Indent at left to next tab stop	Press: **Ctrl + M**	Click: ⊞ on the Formatting Tool Bar	**Format, Paragraph, Indents and Spacing**
Indent at left to previous tab stop	Press: **Ctrl + Shift + M**		
Indent as a hanging paragraph Unindent and return to standard margin	Press: **Ctrl + T** Press: **Ctrl + Q**	Click: ⊞ on the Formatting Tool Bar *Using ruler* first-line indent ▽ left indent ⌂ first-line and left indent ▽⌂ right indent △	
Insert special character/symbols	To change the selection to symbol font: Press: **Ctrl + Shift + Q**		To insert a symbol: Position cursor: Where you want the character/symbol to appear: Select: **Insert, Symbol**
Insert text	Simply key in the missing character(s) at the appropriate place – the existing text will 'move over' to make room for the new text. If **OVR** is displayed (overtyping), Press: **Ins(ert)** key to remove		
Italics	Press: **Ctrl + I**	Click: *I* on the Formatting Tool Bar	**Format, Font**
Justified right margin	Press: **Ctrl + J**	Click: ▤ on the Formatting Tool Bar	**Format, Paragraph, Indents and Spacing, Alignment, Justified**
Line break (to insert)	Press: **Shift + ↵**		
Line length – to change	Select text. Display horizontal ruler. Move margin markers to required position on ruler		
Line spacing – to set	Press: **Ctrl + 1** (single) Press: **Ctrl + 2** (double) Press: **Ctrl + 0** (to add or delete a line space)		**Format, Paragraph, Indents and Spacing, Line Spacing**
Margins (to change)	Use the mouse pointer to drag the left and/or right margin boundaries to the appropriate place on the horizontal ruler. Press: The **Alt** key at the same time to view the measurements on screen		**File, Page Setup, Margins**

Action	Keyboard	Mouse	Menu
Move around document	*See*: Cursor movement		
Move a block of text Select: Text to be moved	Press: **F2 + Ctrl + X**	Click: ✂ on the Standard Tool Bar	**Edit**, **Cut**
Position cursor where text is to be moved to	Press: **Ctrl + V** *or* ↵	Click: 📋 on the Standard Tool Bar *drag and drop moving:* Select: Text to be moved Click: Left mouse button in middle of text and keep held down Drag: Selection to required location Release: Mouse button	*or* Press: Right mouse button; Select: **Cut** Press: Right mouse button; Select: **Paste**
Open an existing file	Press: **Ctrl + O**	Click: 📂 on the Standard Tool Bar	**File**, **Open**
Open a new file	Press: **Ctrl + N**	Click: 🗋 on the Standard Tool Bar	**File**, **New**
Page break (to insert)	Press: **Ctrl + ↵**		**Insert**, **Break**, **Page break**
Page numbering	Press: **Alt + Shift + P**		**Insert**, **Page Numbers**
Page Setup			**File**, **Page Setup** Choose from **Margins**, **Paper Size**, **Paper Source** and **Layout**
Paragraphs – splitting/joining	Make a new paragraph (i.e. split a paragraph into two): Move cursor to first letter of new paragraph: Press ↵ twice Join two consecutive paragraphs into one: Move cursor to first letter of new paragraph: Press ← (**Del**) twice (backspace delete key) Press: **Space Bar** (to insert a space after full stop)		
Print out hard copy	Press: **Ctrl + P**	Click: 🖨 on the Standard Tool Bar	**File**, **Print**
Print Preview	Press: **Ctrl + F2**	Click: 🔍 on the Standard Tool Bar	**File**, **Print Preview**
Select: **Zoom** *or* **Full Page**			
Ragged right margin	Press: **Ctrl + L**	Click: ☰ on the Formatting Tool Bar	**Format**, **Paragraph**, **Indents and Spacing**, **Alignment**, **Left**
Remove text emphasis First, select the emphasised text to be changed back to normal text	Press: **Ctrl + Space Bar** *or* Press: **Ctrl + Shift + Z**	Click: Appropriate emphasis button on the Formatting Tool Bar (to deselect)	**Format**, **Paragraph**, **Indents and Spacing**
Repeat typing or actions (redo)	Press: **F4** to repeat previous action *or* Press: **Ctrl + Y**	Click: ↻ on the Formatting Tool Bar To redo (repeat) sets of actions, drag down the **Redo** drop-down list: Select: The group of actions you wish to repeat	**Edit**, **Repeat Typing**

Replace text – typeover	1 Select: The incorrect text and then type in the correct entry – Word will fit the replacement text exactly into the original space
	2 Move cursor: To incorrect entry:
	   Press: The **Ins** key (typeover on) and overtype with correct entry
	   Press: The **Ins** key again (typeover off) to stop overtyping of text		

Restore deleted text	Press: **Ctrl + Z**	Click: ↺ on the Formatting Tool Bar	**Edit**, **Undo Typing**
Ruler – to display			**View**, **Ruler**
Save work to disk Save a file for the first time	Press: **F12**		**File**, **Save As**, **Enter Filename** Select: Correct Directory/Drive; Click: **OK**

Action	Keyboard	Mouse	Menu
Save an active file which has been saved previously	Press: **Ctrl + S** *or* Press: **Shift + F12**	Click: 💾 on the Standard Tool Bar	**File**, **Save**
Save all open files			**File**, **Save All**
Scroll bars (to view)			**Tools**, **Options**, **View** Select: Horizontal Scroll Bar and Vertical Scroll Bar options
Search for text	*See* Find text		
Select text One character (or more) One word To end of line Start of line A full line A paragraph Whole document Any block of text	Press: **Shift** + → *or* ← Press: **Shift + Ctrl** + → *or* ← Press: **Shift + End** Press: **Shift + Home** Press: **Shift + End** *or* **Home** — Press: **Ctrl + A** —	Click and drag: Pointer across text Double-click: On word Click and drag: Pointer right or down Click and drag: Pointer left or up Click: In selection border Double-click: In selection border Triple-click: In selection border Position pointer: At start of text and Hold down: **Shift**. Then, position pointer at end of text and click	
Remove selection		Click: In any white space	
Spaced capitals	Press: **Caps Lock** key. Leave one space after each letter. Leave three spaces after each word		
Spellcheck	Press: **F7**	Click: ✓ on the Standard Tool Bar	**Tools**, **Spelling and Grammar**
Status Bar			**Tools**, **Options**, **View** Select: Status Bar option
Switch on and load Word		Double-click: **Microsoft Word Icon**	Select: **MS Word from Start**
Symbols	*See* Inserting special characters/symbols		
Tables Insert table		Click: ▦ on the Standard Tool Bar	**Table**, **Insert Table**
Tables and borders		Click: 🗗 on the Standard Tool Bar	**Table**, **Draw Table**
Replace text	Press: **Ctrl + H**		**Edit**, **Replace**
Underline text Single underline Double underline	Press: **Ctrl + U** Press: **Ctrl + Shift + W** Press: **Ctrl + Shift + D**	Click: **U** on the Formatting Tool Bar	**Format**, **Font**, **Underline**
Undo mistakes, typing or actions	Press: **Ctrl + Z**	Click: ↰ on the Standard Tool Bar To undo sets of actions, drag down the **Undo** drop-down list; select: The group of actions you wish to undo	**Edit**, **Undo Typing**
Units of measurement			**Tools**, **Options**, **General**, **Measurement Units** Select: Desired unit from drop-down menu
View magnified pages		Click: 100% on the Standard Tool Bar Click: **Magnifies** on Print Preview	**View**, **Zoom**
View – normal view	Press: **Ctrl + F2**	Click: the ▭ Normal **Normal View** button at left of document window	**View**, **Normal**
View – online view		Click: the ▭ Online L **Online View** button at left of document window	**View**, **Online**
View – outline view		Click: the ▭ Outline **Outline View** button at left of document window	**View**, **Outline**
View – page layout view		Click: the ▣ Page Layout **Page Layout View** button at left of document window	**View**, **Page Layout**
View – Print Preview	Press: **Ctrl + F2**	Click: 🔍 on the Standard Tool Bar	**File**, **Print Preview** Select: **Zoom** or **Full Page**
Widow/orphan control			**Format**, **Paragraph**, **Line and Page Breaks**

Print-out checks

Unit 1
Exercise 1A

A word processor allows text to be created and printed quickly and accurately. Text can be stored on disk or in a directory for future use. You can recall text and modify or rearrange it if you want to make changes without having to type it out again. The ability to edit text should save paper as printing can be done only when the document is perfect.

Two advantages of word processing have been increased productivity and more efficient use of resources. Improvements in printer technology have enabled high-quality text to be attractively produced at great speeds.

Word Processors are often used for general office correspondence such as letters and memos. However, the advantages of the technology are perhaps demonstrated to best effect in the production of reports. Such documents are often long and need to be revised several times. Functions such as headers, automatic page numbering and spelling checks are of great assistance to the operator. Many office workers can now prepare their own reports without having to use the services of an operator.

Mailmerge allows letters to be combined with names and addresses to produce documents, which appear to be personal to the recipient. Companies can send out a mail shot to prospective customers using this facility.

Unit 2
Exercise 2B

Your name

INTRODUCTION TO WORD PROCESSING

A word processor allows text to be created and printed quickly and accurately. Text can be stored on disk or in a directory for future use. You can recall text and modify or rearrange it if you want to make changes without having to type it out again. The ability to edit text should save paper as printing can be done only when the document is perfect.

In the past, typists spent a considerable amount of time in re-typing documents that needed to be amended. Sometimes, a large part of a document had to be re-typed because deleting or adding text altered the page numbering and layout.

Word Processors are often used for general office correspondence such as letters and memos. However, the advantages of the technology are perhaps demonstrated to best effect in the production of reports. Such documents are often long and need to be revised several times. Functions such as headers, automatic page numbering and spelling checks are of great assistance to the operator. Many office workers can now prepare their own reports without having to use the services of an operator.

Two advantages of word processing have been increased productivity and efficient use of resources. Improvements in technology have enabled high-quality text to be produced at great speeds.

Mailmerge allows letters to be combined with names and addresses to produce documents, which appear to be personal to the recipient. Companies can send out a mail shot to prospective customers using this facility.

INTRODUCTION TO WORD PROCESSING

Your name

INTRODUCTION TO WORD PROCESSING

A word processor allows text to be created and printed quickly and accurately. Text can be stored on disk or in a directory for future use. You can recall text and modify or rearrange it if you want to make changes without having to type it out again. The ability to edit text should save paper as printing can be done only when the document is perfect.

In the past, typists spent a considerable amount of time in re-typing documents that needed to be amended. Sometimes, a large part of a document had to be re-typed because deleting or adding text altered the page numbering and layout.

Word Processors are often used for general office correspondence such as letters and memos. However, the advantages of the technology are perhaps demonstrated to best effect in the production of reports. Such documents are often long and need to be revised several times. Functions such as headers, automatic page numbering and spelling checks are of great assistance to the operator. Many office workers can now prepare their own reports without having to use the services of an operator.

Two advantages of word processing have been increased productivity and efficient use of resources. Improvements in technology have enabled high-quality text to be produced at great speeds.

Mailmerge allows letters to be combined with names and addresses to produce documents, which appear to be personal to the recipient. Companies can send out a mail shot to prospective customers using this facility.

INTRODUCTION TO WORD PROCESSING

Your name

INTRODUCTION TO WORD PROCESSING

A word processor allows text to be created and printed quickly and accurately. Text can be stored on disk or in a directory for future use. You can recall text and modify or rearrange it if you want to make changes without having to type it out again. The ability to edit text should save paper as printing can be done only when the document is perfect.

In the past, typists spent a considerable amount of time in re-typing documents that needed to be amended. Sometimes, a large part of a document had to be re-typed because deleting or adding text altered the page numbering and layout

Word Processors are often used for general office correspondence such as letters and memos. However, the advantages of the technology are perhaps demonstrated to best effect in the production of reports. Such documents are often long and need to be revised several times Functions such as headers, automatic page numbering and spelling checks are of great assistance to the operator. Many office workers can now prepare their own reports without having to use the services of an operator.

Two advantages of word processing have been increased productivity and efficient use of resources. Improvements in technology have enabled high-quality text to be produced at great speeds.

Mailmerge allows letters to be combined with names and addresses to produce documents, which appear to be personal to the recipient. Companies can send out a mail shot to prospective customers using this facility

INTRODUCTION TO WORD PROCESSING

Hellebores of the Family Ranunculaceae

This popular English garden plant brightens the colourless months of winter. Delicate cup-shaped flowers, in shades of dark purple to dusky pink and primrose yellow to white, hang from foliage which often doubles as a superb evergreen soil cover.

Some types of hellebores will thrive in the most awkward dry shady places, but they cannot stand being waterlogged. It is possible to propagate hellebores by division around September but many types of hellebores are very generous self-seeders. Each seedling will differ slightly from its parent and could provide a distinct new variety.

Professional breeders continually search for significant differences that can be developed to create new flowers. All parts of the plant are poisonous and even the sap is irritant so it is advisable to wear gloves for protection when handling. Some species of hellebores can cause facial deformities in the offspring of animals that eat the plant.

Line spacing: single and double

In Word 97, you can format the text to appear in double-line spacing (i.e. one blank line between each line of text).

This paragraph is formatted to double-line spacing, which is another method of emphasis and is used to highlight a particular portion of text. Draft documents are often produced in this spacing so that amendments can be easily marked.

Sometimes, in double-line spacing, it is very difficult to tell where one paragraph ends and another starts if the last line of the first paragraph is a long one. For example can you tell that there is a new paragraph at the beginning of the 5th line of text – the one beginning 'Sometimes, in double-line spacing . . .'?

A paragraph in double-line spacing format looks better if it has an extra line space above and below it (as in the example shown here). This 'separates' the paragraph from others in single-line spacing.

When working in double-line spacing, if you press the Return key twice at the end of a sentence as usual, there will be *three* clear lines between each paragraph. When you are changing line spacing for sections of a document during editing, you may find that line spacing between paragraphs becomes inconsistent. In an examination, consistency of presentation is important and you should always check through your document and correct any inconsistencies in line spacing before printing.

Hellebores of the Family Ranunculaceae

This popular English garden plant brightens the colourless months of

winter. Delicate cup-shaped blooms, in shades of dark purple to dusky

pink and primrose yellow to white, hang from foliage which often

doubles as a superb evergreen soil cover.

Some varieties of hellebores will thrive in the most awkward dry shady places, but they cannot stand being waterlogged. It is possible to propagate hellebores by division around September but many varieties of hellebores are very generous self-seeders. Each seedling will differ slightly from its parent and could provide a distinct new variety.

Professional growers continually search for significant differences that can be developed to create new blooms. All parts of the plant are poisonous and even the sap is irritant so it is advisable to wear gloves for protection when handling. Some species of hellebores can cause facial deformities in the offspring of animals that eat the plant

Your name

BENEFITS OF WORD PROCESSING

A word processor allows text to be created and printed quickly and accurately. Text can be stored on disk or in a directory for future use. You can recall text and modify or rearrange it if you want to make changes without having to type it out again. The ability to edit text should save paper as printing can be done only when the document is perfect.

In the past, typists spent a considerable amount of time in re-typing documents

that needed to be amended. Sometimes, a large part of a document had to be

re-typed because deleting or adding text altered the page numbering and layout.

Word Processors are frequently used for general office correspondence such as letters and memos. However, the advantages of the technology are perhaps demonstrated to best effect in the production of reports. Such documents are frequently long and need to be revised several times. Functions such as headers, automatic page numbering and spelling checks are of great assistance to the operator. Many office workers can now prepare their own reports without having to use the services of an operator.

Two advantages of word processing have been increased productivity and efficient use of resources. Improvements in technology have enabled high-quality text to be generated at great speeds.

Mailmerge allows letters to be combined with names and addresses to generate documents which appear to be personal to the recipient. Companies can send out a mail shot to prospective customers using this facility

BENEFITS OF WORD PROCESSING

Better Business Services Ltd

43 Accringley Vale Road
BRADFORD BD11 3GT
Tel no: 01274 729372
Fax no: 01274 729373

VAT No. 935 4789 20
Registered in England No. 949 8856

Better Business Services Ltd

MEMORANDUM

Unit 6
Exercise 6B

COMMUNICATIONS

It may be 'good to talk' but is it always cheap? If you dial out from a hotel telephone to communicate the answer could be different from what you think. In America, many hotels will charge customers for calls even if they are unable to get through! Hotel telephone charges vary, but one survey revealed that many hotels add between 400% and 800% more than a home based call.

Customers have complained that it would be cheaper to use their mobile telephones than to use the hotel's telephone facilities.

Following the barrage of angry complaints, some hotels are now relaxing their rules as they realise that the profit made on inflated telephone charges is being negated through loss of repeat custom.

Another major cause of customer concern has been the practice of some hotels in making a charge for what are usually freephone numbers.

Some hotels are reversing the trend and charging for the cost of the call only, but many previously bitten customers now take one of the national telephone charge cards with them as a precaution.

Unit 5
Exercise 5E

Draft copy

MAYTON VALE CHOIR

AUTUMN PROGRAMME

Fit As A Fiddle
You Are My Lucky Star
All I Do Is Dream Of You
(Singin' In The Rain)

I Got Rhythm
Someone To Watch Over Me
Nice Work If You Can Get It
(Crazy For You)

Any Dream Will Do
Close Every Door To Me
One More Angel
(Joseph And The Amazing Technicolor Dreamcoat)

MAYTON VILLAGE HALL
WEDNESDAY 20 OCTOBER 1998, 7.30 PM
ALL SEATS £2.50

HISTORY OF ADVERTISING AND MEDIA EXPANSION

Advertising has been around for many centuries, and can be traced back to the days of ancient Greece, where historians found the first clear evidence of advertising being used for commercial purposes.

The first signs of media expansion developed through printing in the second half of the 15th century which offered a whole new dimension.

However, it was not until the end of the Industrial Revolution (late 18th century) that advertising began to really establish itself. By the 20th century a massive media expansion was making its impact on society.

During the 19th century, a number of factors combined to stimulate the growth of advertising in Britain. One of the most important was the development of large industrial companies putting the mass output theories of Adam Smith into practice, and using economies of scale (buying raw materials in bulk at a cheaper price) to turn out massive quantities of goods at a lower unit price.

In order to maintain the output of such large quantities of food, soap, clothing and other items, these firms needed to develop mass consumption as well as mass output.

The best way of doing this, since they could not afford to employ enough salesmen to sell to the whole population in person, was by advertising.

This led to the development of the most important single medium for the communication of ideas, opinions, knowledge and advertisements - the newspaper. The newspaper was the first recognised modern mass medium.

ADMINISTRATIVE WORK

Every organisation has to keep records and communicate. Businesses depend upon each other for their success and the inefficiency of one can affect many others. Within a company, administrative workers are responsible for ensuring that all processes run smoothly. Each individual within an organisation has internal customers - people or departments who rely on them for information.

If you enjoy keeping things in order, planning your workload, and paying attention to detail, you have the basic skills to become an administrator. Most of the work is carried out indoors with the use of computers. You need to be able to get on well with other people, not just customers but your colleagues too. You can take pride in doing a job well and providing efficient and vital support to the organisation which employs you.

Some administrative work is routine but, at a supervisory level, it becomes very complex and requires a flexible mature attitude and the ability to make decisions quickly. It is important to be observant and to enjoy meeting challenges.

A group of local business owners has recently made definite plans for the development of a new business park in the town. They believe that there is an increasing need for a complex of this type and have researched sites where such a development could be accommodated. After looking through the advertisements of specialist consultants, they have definitely decided to employ a team of experts who they believe will be able to continue this research. In the near future, they hope to receive the recommendations of this team.

In recommending a particular site, the consultants have been requested to develop the idea of incorporating a hotel and leisure business, which could offer accommodation for visiting business people and also for tourists. As the town is located on the fringes of a national park, the group believes that business and leisure interests can be developed together and each would receive benefit through the activities and advertising of the other.

HEALTH AND SAFETY AT WORK

When you first start working for an organisation, you will take part in an induction

programme. In a small company, this may be carried out by your immediate superior

and be quite informal. In a large organisation, you may join induction training along

with other new employees.

You will be given information on risk assessment. You may have to submit a report to

the Health and Safety Representative. It is the responsibility of both the employer and

the employee to ensure a safe working environment. Where more than 5 people are

employed, it is necessary to have a safety policy and to implement it. Safety

representatives form a Safety committee to monitor all aspects

---

It is possible that when you apply for a post as a secretary, you may find it necessary to

obtain a reference from a previous employer or from your College tutor. Any

organisation which is recruiting new staff will take every opportunity to find out as

much as possible about prospective candidates.

A reference will provide valuable information on your skills and abilities and, if you

have just left College, the Personnel Department may refer to your tutor for details of

your previous year's work. Your examination successes will show your achievements,

ie passes or distinctions in word processing, information technology etc.

MEETING TO COMMUNICATE

Organisations use meetings as a method of communicating between employees and with shareholders. The Articles of Association of a company may allow the Board of Directors to set up committees to perform certain tasks and then to report back to the Board. For example, an Advisory Committee could make recommendations but is not empowered to make binding decisions. A Standing Committee meets regularly and is a permanent group. Ad Hoc Committees are set up to achieve a particular purpose and then disbanded. Executive Committees have the power to make binding decisions within their terms of reference (intra vires).

Sometimes it is necessary to form a Sub-Committee for a special purpose. A Joint Committee co-ordinates the work of other committees. Sub-Committees and Joint Committees may be 'standing' or 'ad hoc'.

Formal meetings must be quorate, ie the minimum number of members (the quorum) must be present. Proposals put to the meeting are usually called 'motions'. After discussion, a resolution is passed by voting. The Chairperson can discontinue (adjourn) a meeting and, if no date is set for its continuance, the adjournment is said to be 'sine die'.

FACING THE INTERFACE

Technological innovation has revolutionised business systems and procedures. Jargon words have crept into our vocabulary although terms such as mainframe, laptop and Internet are generally understood nowadays. If you are required to become involved in the purchase of computer hardware or software, you will have to undertake extensive research or refer to specialist consultants.

There are many factors to be considered when buying hardware: processing speed, memory size, pixels, peripherals etc. Operating systems programs such as Windows and OS/2 use a Graphical User Interface; DOS uses a textual interface. The icons you are learning to use in this book are examples of a Graphical User Interface. Fortunately, you do not have to know this to be able to use software such as Word for Windows!

Although you are inputting data into your computer using the keyboard and the mouse, there are many other input devices such as bar-code readers, light pens, document readers and digitisers. Digitisers allow drawings and photographs to be displayed on a monitor.

TRANSPORT IN THE INDUSTRIAL REVOLUTION

The Industrial Revolution greatly increased the demand for coal, iron and other raw materials Roads at the time were often little more than rutted tracks - not suitable for the transportation of goods in bulk The eighteenth century saw the building of canals across the country This method of carrying goods, still using horse-drawn vessels, was usually faster than by road

The use of water courses was not a new idea The Romans, Chinese and Persians also used canals

The working life of the canals was rather short as railways provided a much swifter method of moving raw materials and manufactured goods Railways began to be built in the latter half of the nineteenth century, and canals are now used more for leisure than for business

FOLLOWING HOUSE STYLE

When you start working for a new organisation, you may have to make amendments to the way in which you have previously prepared documents Most companies have adopted a 'house style' for their documents, particularly letters This ensures that there is a uniform presentation style for everything that leaves the office

If you are not sure of the house style, look in the files or folders you are using You should find copies of documents previously used In most cases, you will find that there is a 'template' on your word processor You can simply retrieve this and enter the details in the appropriate places The use of templates saves a considerable amount of time as well as ensuring uniformity

The style of presentation may be different from what you have learned and you may not like it - but it may have been designed for a specific purpose and you will have to adopt the house style or your work will not be usable

BUSINESS EXHIBITION

On Wednesday of next week, we intend to follow your advice and take the opportunity of visiting the exhibition you recommended in our discussions last year We have advertised our organisation in many business publications, giving information on the development of our products in all possible areas

Your organisation has encouraged us to believe in the power of advertising and we have made a definite commitment to promoting our high-quality accommodation in this country and abroad We hope to receive positive feedback from our secretaries who will be enjoying the opportunity of meeting possible future customers at the exhibition

CANALS - PAST AND PRESENT

A talk by Dr James Arkwright
of the STATON CIVIC TRUST

Tickets £2.00   Concessions £1.50
Book at Staton Library or Post Office

STATON CIVIC CENTRE

Monday 25 April
8 pm

Refreshments

BOOK EARLY - TICKETS ARE LIMITED

Your notice may be different from this example but, provided you have copied the text accurately and followed instructions, your display will be acceptable.

New Appointments

The recent major review of our organisation has identified a definite need to recruit more administrators   The increase in our sales and customer service functions means that it will be necessary to appoint new people for our Call Centre

The persons appointed should practise an efficient way of working and possess excellent communication skills   Companies are judged by first impressions and by the after-sales service they provide.   A courteous response and prompt action by individuals empowered to deal with problems are both factors which lead to satisfied customers

We have made preliminary arrangements for the training of staff by a specialist team   Product knowledge will be extensively covered by our own Company trainers during induction sessions.

Our Human Resource Manager, with the help of colleagues on the Customer Service Department, is currently working on press advertisements

Joseph Dean
26 Newley Road
HALIFAX
HX1 3PQ

Today's date

Mrs Fellows
39 Endersby Crescent
SHEFFIELD
SH9 2UZ

Dear Mrs Fellows

I am sending you this letter to show you the new style of personal letter writing which I have been taught on my business course. As you can see, no punctuation is used in the addresses, the date, the salutation or the complimentary close. (Punctuation is only used in the body of the letter to make sure that it makes sense.)

Have you noticed how all the lines start at the left margin? This is called the 'fully blocked' style - if you try it you will see that it is a much quicker method than the 'indentation' style. It is normal practice to use single line-spacing for the paragraphs and leave one clear line between paragraphs.

As you are looking for new employment, I thought it may be useful for you to study the layout of this letter and use it as a model for your new job applications. A well laid out covering letter can make a good first impression on prospective employers.

Yours sincerely

Joseph Dean (Mr)

The Ebony Club
45 Marton Crescent
WAKEFIELD
WF5 3RT

Today's date

Mary Wadsworth
12 New Street
WAKEFIELD
WF4 9EW

Dear Mary

I am writing to thank you for your excellent presentation at the Ebony Club last Thursday evening.

I have received several requests from our committee enquiring if it would be possible for you to make a return visit in about six months' time when we will be holding our annual open evening.

I will forward more information about the evening when this becomes available. The date for your diary is 16 October 1998 - we shall probably begin around 8.00 pm.

Could you please let my secretary have your bank details so that we can settle your fee in full? Payment will be made according to our agreed rate.

I have recommended you to several other organisations that I believe would benefit from your services.

Yours sincerely

Steven Bentley (Mr)

ASSOCIATION OF PERSONAL ASSISTANTS

**Visit to Head Office of
the STATON & WOODFORD TIMES**

Thursday 12 March at 7.00 pm

Tour of new premises

Talk by Miss B Bridge, Secretary to Editor

Presentation: Technology in Journalism Today

Buffet supper provided

Meet at Woodford House, Staton Road, Woodford
at 6.45 pm

Your notice may be different from this example but, provided you have copied the text accurately and followed instructions, your display will be acceptable.

Worth House
Aire Street
STATON
N Yorkshire
NY6 3GE

(Date of typing)

Miss J M Pinfold
3 Derby Road
STATON
N Yorkshire
NY12 4LD

Dear Miss Pinfold

Thank you for returning the membership application form.

I understand that you are interested in becoming a full member of the Association and I am pleased to confirm that your references have been checked by our committee and they have given their approval to your application.

Please let us have your cheque for the annual subscription fee of £30. This should be sent to Mrs C Rollinson, Secretary to the Association at the above address

Our meetings are held at Worth House, Aire Street, on the second Thursday of each month. A full programme giving information on speakers and visits will be sent to you as soon as possible

I would like to take this opportunity to welcome you to the Association and hope that you will enjoy our activities.

Yours sincerely

Rosemary Caton

WHO DOES WHAT?

A company's organisation chart shows internal structure and lines of responsibility. The chart looks rather like a family tree and usually shows a hierarchical structure.

The span of control of individual managers sets out the person to whom each employee is responsible. It is important that the chart both stipulates and reflects effective lines of communication within a company. Many problems are caused by poor or inadequate communications procedures.

Another vital document for employees is the job description - their own and other people's. This should clearly outline the following information:

Job Title
Department
Objectives
Responsibilities
Person(s) accountable for
Person(s) accountable to

The job description is normally sent to prospective applicants, together with a person specification which gives details of qualifications, skills and qualities considered essential or desirable for the postholder. Applicants should carefully match their own capabilities with the person specification.

Job descriptions and organisation charts lay the foundations for ensuring good communications and efficient operations. All employees need to take account of the company's published documents, eg policies on equal opportunities, health and safety etc as these help to determine each employee's individual role and responsibilities, in addition to those relating to the specific post shown in their job description.

ORGANISING YOUR WORKSTATION

Whether your working office is large and open-plan or small and private, it needs to be organised so that you can work efficiently and comfortably. The furniture may be out of your control but it may be possible to suggest improvements when the right time comes along!

Try to keep the desk surface as tidy as possible so that you can spread out when you need to do written work. Secretaries should use a copy-holder when they are keying in and make sure that they sit properly on a well-designed chair.

Develop the habit of placing loose papers in folders with a definite label such as 'To do' or 'To read'. It may not be possible to handle each document only once as some business managers recommend but the strategy of using folders reduces the risk of losing papers.

If you are organised, you will then be able to locate information necessary for your job. Anyone looking at your desk and working areas will feel that you are efficient and a credit to your organisation. Some people believe that a tidy desk shows a tidy mind!

MAKING APPLICATION

The letter

As with any correspondence for which you are responsible, your letter of application should show that you appreciate the need for good presentation and complete accuracy. Do not add your signature to a letter if it is not sufficiently good. Signing a letter makes you responsible for its content. The advertisement in the newspaper probably requested good business and administrative skills such as checking and proof-reading!

On receipt of letters of application, experienced personnel assess them, separating some to draw up a 'short list' of approximately six applicants who are judged to have sufficient necessary experience for the advertised post.

Unfortunately, some companies do not send any acknowledgement to unsuccessful applicants, perhaps because the financial expense is great. Applicants are left waiting for correspondence, having gone to the expense of submitting an application. Applying for even one post takes a considerable amount of time. It can be inconvenient when applicants are in the position of having to make a definite decision about taking a post without having information on other applications they have made.

Additional information

A letter of application may need a separate application form or curriculum vitae. Specific information may be requested, eg

Work history - temporary and permanent posts held
Experience of liaising with clients and colleagues
Foreign language competence
Qualifications and attainments
Education

You may sometimes see that an advertisement informs applicants that they should assume they have been unsuccessful if they have not heard from the company within a given period of time.

WHO DOES WHAT?

A company's organisation chart shows the internal structure and lines of responsibility. The chart looks rather like a family tree and usually shows a hierarchical structure.

The span of control of individual managers sets out the person to whom each employee is responsible. It is important that the chart both directs and reflects effective lines of communication within a company. Many problems are caused by poor or inadequate communications procedures.

Organisation charts lay the foundations for ensuring good communications and efficient operations. All employees need to take account of the company's published documents, eg policies on equal opportunities, health and safety etc as these help to determine each employee's individual role and responsibilities, in addition to those relating to their specific post.

Another vital document for employees is the job description - their own and others. This should clearly outline the following information.

Job Title
Department
Objectives
Responsibilities
Person(s) accountable to
Person(s) accountable for

The job description is normally sent to prospective applicants, together with a job specification which gives details of qualifications, skills and qualities considered essential or desirable for the postholder. Applicants should carefully match their own capabilities with the job specification.

MAKING A JOB APPLICATION

The letter

On receipt of letters of application, experienced personnel assess them, separating some to draw up a 'short list' of approximately six applicants who are judged to have sufficient necessary experience for the advertised post.

As with any correspondence for which you are responsible, your letter of application should show that you appreciate the need for good presentation and complete accuracy. Do not add your signature to a letter if it is not of an acceptable standard. Signing a letter makes you responsible for its content. The advertisement in the newspaper probably requested good business and administrative skills such as checking and proof-reading!

Unfortunately, some companies do not send any acknowledgement to unsuccessful applicants, perhaps because the financial expense is great. Applicants are left waiting for correspondence, having gone to the expense of submitting an application. Applying for even one post takes a considerable amount of time. It can be inconvenient when applicants are in the position of having to make a definite decision about taking a post without having feedback on other applications they have made.

You may sometimes see that an advertisement informs applicants that they should assume they have been unsuccessful if they have not heard from the company within a given period of time.

Additional information

A letter of application may need a separate application form or curriculum vitae. Specific information may be requested, eg

Work history - temporary and permanent posts held
Experience of liaising with clients and colleagues
Foreign language competence
Education
Qualifications and attainments

Better Business Services Ltd

MEMORANDUM

FROM: Dave Mills, PREMISES MANAGER
TO: Madeleine Yeats, PERSONNEL OFFICER
DATE: today's
REF: DM/011491

STAFF SHORTAGES

In relation to the brief discussion we had last week about the shortage of accommodation staff, I have now drafted a job description for the two temporary positions which should alleviate the situation until we are able to recruit permanent staff. I am still collecting all the information needed to assess how many additional permanent staff the organisation will need for necessary maintenance standards.

I would appreciate your comments on appropriate salary scales before the end of next week, if possible. There may be an opportunity to discuss this issue at our meeting tomorrow.

I have received the draft induction policy for new staff which you circulated last week. I think it is definitely a step in the right direction.

It would also be helpful if you could let me have a copy of the new salary scales which will come into force next year.

Better Business Services Ltd

MEMORANDUM

FROM: Madeleine Yeats, PERSONNEL OFFICER
TO: Dave Mills, PREMISES MANAGER
DATE: today's
REF: MY/00ZA2

ACCOMMODATION STAFF

The advertisement for two temporary accommodation staff will go into the local paper next Friday evening. It should be possible to hold interviews two weeks later and I plan to reserve the morning of Wednesday 26 October for this purpose. I trust this date will not be inconvenient for you.

I will forward the applications and any copies of references to you a week prior to this date for your initial screening.

Copies of the new salary scales for next year are not available at the moment. However, I am pleased to advise that the induction policy has been finalised and published and will, therefore, be available for the new members of your team.

Better Business Services Ltd
43 Accringley Vale Road
BRADFORD BD11 3GT
Tel no: 01274 2249317
Fax no: 01274 2249313
VAT No. 935 4789 20
Registered in England No. 949 8856

Our ref: MY/00za9

today's date

CONFIDENTIAL

Mr B Shields
33 Randolph Avenue
BRADFORD
BD19 3TU

Dear Mr Shields

Position of Accommodations Officer (Temporary)

I am pleased to advise you that you have been shortlisted for the position of Accommodations Officer (Temporary). Although this is initially a temporary post, it is envisaged that the successful candidate will continue in the role, subject to mutually acceptable conditions, when it is made permanent in approximately six months' time.

We intend to hold interviews on the morning of Wednesday, 26 October.

We will begin at 9.30 am with an introductory tour of the company. This will be followed by coffee and an opportunity to meet other members of the team. Your actual interview before the panel is scheduled for 11.15 am. Please find enclosed a stamped, addressed envelope for your reply and a form on which to claim any travel expenses. I would be grateful if you would confirm that you can attend on the date indicated.

Yours sincerely

Madeleine Yeats
PERSONNEL OFFICER

Encs

Better Business Services Ltd

MEMORANDUM

From   Cathy Potterton   Training Officer

To   All Unit Supervisors and Section Heads

Ref   CP/TO/2703

Date   *Date of typing*

I would like to invite you to a half-day Seminar which is to take place at Head Office, 43 Accringley Vale Road, BRADFORD BD11 3GT.

The Seminar will be held in Room 201 on Thursday 27 March from 9.30 am to approximately 12.30 pm. Refreshments will be provided on arrival.

I enclose a copy of the Seminar programme which briefly outlines the content and gives the names of the speakers.

You will no doubt agree that the issues to be discussed are very important for the health of the workforce and productivity of our business It is anticipated that all Supervisors and Section Heads will arrange to pass on the information to their teams at briefing sessions as soon as possible **This should take place within three weeks**

Please take this opportunity to become informed about company policies prior to the new legislation coming into force. Complete the booking form attached with your details and signature, and return to my secretary, Lana Knightley.

Encs

Better Business Services Ltd

43 Accringley Vale Road
BRADFORD BD11 3GT
Tel no: 01274 224937/2
Fax no: 01274 224937/3

VAT No 935 4 789 20
Registered in England No 549 8856

Our ref: CC/00439

today's date

URGENT

Mr D Singh
223 Brook Road
SHIPLEY
BD18 4TR

Dear Mr Singh

Order No: RT297

Thank you for your letter which I received today I was most concerned to note that you had been unable to deliver the consignment of office furniture, ordered by our company, due to delays in your production.

We have several new secretaries commencing employment with us next month for whom the furniture is required to be in place. Unless you are able to guarantee a definite delivery date within the next 7 days I am afraid we shall have no choice but to cancel our order and close our account with you.

I would appreciate it if you would contact me within the next 2 days to advise me of your position. In anticipation of an early delivery, I would also suggest that you liaise with our Premises Manager, Dave Mills, who will make any further necessary arrangements. I enclose his business card for your reference.

Yours sincerely

Jenny Davidson (Ms)
PURCHASING MANAGER

Enc

Better Business Services Ltd

**43 Accringley Vale Road
BRADFORD BD11 3GT**
Tel no: 01274 224937/2
Fax no: 01274 224937/3

VAT No. 935 4789 20
Registered in England No. 949 8856

Our ref CP/TO/S103

Date of typing

Ms M Simon
Green Park Consultants Ltd
Green Park
CHESTER
CH9 7HQ

Dear Ms Simon

I write to confirm our telephone conversation earlier today when you kindly agreed to be the keynote speaker at our in-house Seminar on Thursday 27 March.

The company places great emphasis on keeping all employees up to date with information concerning legislation which affects their health and, of course, the organisation's livelihood. We are pleased that it is possible for you to pass on your expertise to us despite being contacted at such short notice

I have forwarded details of the Seminar programme to members of our supervisory staff. Approximately 20 places have been reserved for them. The room is equipped with the usual presentation facilities. Please let me know if you have any special requirements

Lunch has been arranged for the main participants and I hope you will join us.

In addition to Seminar details, I also enclose a map giving directions from the nearest exit on the M62, and look forward to meeting you at 9.00 am on the above date

Yours sincerely

Cathy Potterton
Training Officer

Encs

Better Business Services Ltd

**43 Accringley Vale Road
BRADFORD BD11 3GT**
Tel no: 01274 224937/2
Fax no: 01274 224937/3

VAT No. 935 4789 20
Registered in England No. 949 8856

Ref CP/TO/VID

Date of typing

Sales Department
Mega Training PLC
136 Connerton Place
BRADFIELD
BF2 8LC

Dear Sirs

I have received a copy of your current catalogue after discussing our company's training needs with your colleagues at the recent Northern Business Exhibition in Manchester.

We are interested in several of your products and would welcome the opportunity to see examples of your training materials, including worksheets and video presentations. I note from the catalogue that you recommend a visit by one of your representatives

I must point out that our training and seminar accommodation will be temporarily closed for refurbishment **from the end of next month.** It would therefore be more convenient for us to come to your offices during this time. However, it there is sufficient time to arrange the presentation in the very near future, our current facilities would be adequate.

I have completed the necessary request card indicating our particular areas of interest, and look forward to hearing from you. The card is attached to this letter

Yours faithfully

Cathy Potterton
Training Officer

Enc

WORK-RELATED HEALTH

Companies have a statutory duty to provide a safe workplace for their employees and to protect their physical and mental health. The Health and Safety Acts are designed to make this happen.

Stress causes both absenteeism and illness   The most stressful jobs are said to be experienced by those in nursing, social work, the police force, and teaching but the highest level of absenteeism is in manual work. Workers in the financial sector show the lowest rates of absenteeism. Although the use of computers is considered to cause stress in the workplace, it would seem that it is working with people, perhaps within financial and social constraints, that causes the most stress

However, there are many changes which can be made to help reduce stress. The first step is to understand stress and to recognise where and when it is occurring. It may then be possible to provide a more flexible job structure, alternating high and low stress tasks

Counselling can help some people but it may simply be enough for managers and colleagues to listen to problems and respond to them.

Some of the larger organisations now offer relaxation and leisure opportunities to their employees such as gyms, social events, on-site massage, etc. Such facilities encourage people to take a break and to do something which will relieve mental tension and the muscular aches and pains which come with it. This may prove a cost-effective and pleasurable way for employers to maintain health and keep the effects of stress to a minimum.

Better Business Services Ltd

MEMORANDUM

From   Cathy Potterton   Training Officer

To   Shaheen Zaman   Personal Assistant to MD

Ref   CP/TO/SI04

Date   *Date of typing*

We are holding an in-house Seminar in the near future and I have asked my new secretary, Lana Knightley, to liaise with you regarding arrangements for accommodation, equipment, catering etc

As my secretary is new to the company, she feels she would like assistance from an experienced member of staff. You were recommended to us as your work involves dealing with clients, government official and foreign visitors

I did refer my suggestion to Jane Larchwood before writing to you. She agreed to release you for a few hours next week.

We would be grateful if you could help with the financial information, practical details, and all the miscellaneous tasks necessary to the success of such a venture. It would help a new colleague by giving her the opportunity to develop skills and confidence, and would be much appreciated by all concerned

I hope you enjoy the experience of training - I know this area of work is a possible future role you would welcome

Professional growers continually search for significant differences that can be developed to create new blooms. All parts of the plant are poisonous and even the sap is irritant so it is advisable to wear gloves for protection when handling. Some species of hellebores can cause facial deformities in the offspring of animals that eat the plant.

2

<u>Hellebores of the Family Ranunculaceae</u>

This popular English garden plant brightens the colourless months of winter. Delicate cup-shaped blooms, in shades of dark purple to dusky pink and primrose yellow to white, hang from foliage which often doubles as a superb evergreen soil cover.

Some varieties of hellebores will thrive in the most awkward dry shady places, but they cannot stand being waterlogged. It is possible to propagate hellebores by division around September but many varieties of hellebores are very generous self-seeders. Each seedling will differ slightly from its parent and could provide a distinct new variety.

Another major cause of customer concern has been the practice of some hotels in making a charge for what are usually freephone numbers.

Some hotels are reversing the trend and charging for the cost of the call only, but many previously bitten customers now take one of the national telephone charge cards with them as a precaution.

2

COMMUNICATIONS

It may be 'good to talk' but is it always cheap? If you dial out from a hotel telephone to communicate the answer could be different to what you think. In America, many hotels will charge customers for calls even if they are unable to get through! Hotel telephone charges vary, but one survey revealed that many hotels add between 400% to 800% more than a home based call.

Customers have complained that it would be cheaper to use their mobile telephones than to use the hotel's telephone facilities.

Following the barrage of angry complaints, some hotels are now relaxing their rules as they realise that the profit made on inflated telephone charges is being negated through loss of repeat custom.

1

THE BENEFITS OF BRANDING

What is a brand?

The dictionary defines the difference between a product and a brand as follows:

PRODUCT: *result of process of manufacture*
BRAND: *trademark, particular quality (of goods)*

The term 'product' applies to an undifferentiated range of commodities (or services) For example, milk, cheese and eggs are known as dairy products On the other hand, 'Goldenlay' is a unique, identifiable brand of eggs; 'Kraft' is a unique, identifiable brand of cheese.

Brands have a unique name and often their own logo, design and packaging. They may be classified as:

Brand types	Examples
Company brands	Morphy Richards, Dorlux, Panasonic
House brands	Kayes, Burlington, Janet Frazer
	(all belong to the same catalogue firm)
Umbrella brands	Polyfilla, Polycell, Easicell
Individual brands	Kellogg's Cornflakes, Big Mac
Distributors brands	Marks & Spencer
	(distribute St Michael brands)

Advantages of developing a brand

Giving products unique 'personalities' distinguishes them from their competitors. Getting the consumer to recognise benefits and advantages associated with a particular brand represents a considerable long-term investment for the organisation.

An established reputation requires relatively less expenditure than competitors in order to maintain sales. Superior profitability offers more liberal choices in decision-making for future investments in quality improvement of further marketing expenditure. Company take-overs where strong brands exist demonstrate much higher prices being paid.

1

Customer perceptions and brand functions

For a brand to be successful, its identity must be immediately clear. Also, the brand should reflect a summary of information and associations which is triggered off in the consumer's memory. Consumers need to feel secure in their purchase and that the familiar brand guarantees added value such as better quality or better value for money.

Building and maintaining the brand is a central function of marketing and critical to the profitability of the organisation.

2

CUSTOMER PERCEPTIONS AND BRAND FUNCTIONS

For a brand to be successful, its **identity** must be immediately clear. Also, the brand should reflect a **summary of information and associations** which is triggered off in the customer's memory.

Customers need to feel **secure** in their purchase and that the familiar brand guarantees **added value** such as better quality or better value for money. Through continual marketing activity and brand recognition, a more rapid means of memory interrogation minimises information search and evaluation, thereby reducing the effort needed to make the purchase.

Building and maintaining the brand is a central function of marketing and critical to the profitability of the organisation.

2

Your name

THE BENEFITS OF BRANDING

WHAT IS A BRAND?

The dictionary defines the difference between a product and a brand in the following way:

PRODUCT: *result of process of manufacture*
BRAND: *trademark, particular quality (of goods)*

The term 'product' signifies an undifferentiated range of commodities (or services). For example, milk, cheese and eggs are classed as dairy products. On the other hand, 'Goldenlay' is a unique, identifiable brand of eggs; 'Kraft' is a unique, identifiable brand of cheese.

Brands have a unique name and often their own logo, design and packaging. They may be classified as:

Brand types	Ref	Examples
Company	A)	Morphy Richards, Dorlux, Panasonic
House	B)	Kayes, Burlington, Janet Frazer
Umbrella	C)	Polyfilla, Polycell, Easicell
Individual	D)	Kellogg's Cornflakes, Big Mac
Distributors	E)	Marks & Spencer

ADVANTAGES OF DEVELOPING A BRAND

Giving products unique 'personalities' distinguishes them from their competitors. Getting the customer to recognise benefits and advantages associated with a particular brand represents a considerable long-term investment for the organisation.

Some organisations have been so successful in marketing their products that the brand name has become a synonym for the product. For example, 'Flymo' is often used to mean lawn mower.

An established reputation requires relatively less expenditure than competitors in order to maintain sales. Superior profitability offers more liberal choices in decision-making for future investments in quality improvement of further marketing expenditure. Company take-overs where strong brands exist demonstrate much higher prices being paid.

Your name

HISTORY OF ADVERTISING AND MEDIA EXPANSION

Advertising has been around for many centuries, and its origins can be traced back to the days of ancient Greece, where historians found the first clear evidence of advertising being used for commercial purposes.

The first signs of media expansion developed through printing in the latter half of the 15th century which offered a whole new dimension. It was several centuries later, however, towards the end of the Industrial Revolution (late 18th century) that advertising really began to establish itself.

As industry replaced traditional craftsmanship with machine-based mass production, people moved from rural areas into urban areas for the large number of jobs that became available. Towns and cities increased in their population size and house numbers. The new jobs and new houses also needed to be advertised as well as the new products.

During the 19th century, a number of factors

combined to stimulate the expansion of advertising in

Britain. One of the most important was the

development of large industrial companies putting

the mass production theories of Adam Smith into

practice, and using economies of scale to turn out

massive quantities of goods at a lower unit price.

In order to maintain the production of such large quantities of food, soap, clothing and other items, these firms needed to develop mass consumption as well as mass production. If companies were to buy in bulk at cheaper prices, they also needed to sell in bulk to sustain adequate profit margins.

Introduction of the Newspaper

The most effective way of achieving this, since they could not afford to employ enough salesmen to sell to the whole population in person, was by advertising. This led to the development of the most important single medium for the communication of ideas, opinions, knowledge and advertisements - the newspaper.

The newspaper was the first recognised modern mass medium. By the 20th century a massive media expansion was making its impact on society.

Newspapers were not a 19th century invention, although their production, format and readerships changed considerably during that period as they became industrialised.

The Industrial Revolution gave newspapers the kick-

start needed to mature from a form of media that

was only reporting on local stories.

2

Your name

ECONOMIC IMPACT REPORT

The following areas must be addressed by the committee members and a full report of intended activities submitted before the end of the month shown below:

MONTH	AREA OF ACTIVITY
June	Regeneration of areas and industries.
July	Business development and overseas investment.
August	Tourism, transport and the environment.
September	Research and development - scientific and agricultural.

In order to obtain comprehensive and timely information needed for the final report, it is suggested that committee members undertake the areas of responsibility detailed below:

NAME	SPECIALISM	MONTH END
Wayne Anderson	Enterprise	July
Pauline Bretton	Transport Logistics	June
Lavinia de Courcy	Urban Regeneration	June
Margaret Haigh	Environmental Studies	August
Matthew Hart	Business Development	June
Vera Kadinsky	International Trade	June
Samantha Prescott	Research Studies	September
Mohammed Saleed	Industrial development	June
Mark Schmitt	Agriculture	September
Joanne Turner	Travel and Tourism	August
Tim Wetherspoon	Chemical Plant	September
Lewis Young	Green Studies	August

Members should ensure they are able to access word-processing facilities in order to provide their document file on disk as well as hard copy. Marjorie Faulkes, Secretary to the Chairman, will collate each individual report into a final document ready for the next Planning Group meeting.

Your name

PROPOSED AUTUMN PROGRAMME

MAYTON VALE CHOIR

AUTUMN PROGRAMME

I Got Rhythm
Someone To Watch Over Me
Nice Work If You Can Get It
(Crazy For You)

Fit As A Fiddle
You Are My Lucky Star
All I Do Is Dream Of You
(Singin' In The Rain)

One More Angel
Any Dream Will Do
Close Every Door To Me
(Joseph And The Amazing Technicolor Dreamcoat)

MAYTON VILLAGE HALL
WEDNESDAY 20 OCTOBER 1998, 8.00 PM
ALL SEATS £2.50

The Choir will put on a special production in the Autumn with a selection of songs from three popular Broadway shows. TICKETS ARE ALREADY SELLING WELL! Rehearsals are going well and members feel that this will be the best show ever.

The costumes for the show are being made by the local college who run several courses in fashion design. We have agreed to pay the college a small percentage of the profits to cover the cost of materials, and to include them on our advertising literature. This is a small price to pay for the excellent service being offered.

We have also been fortunate in securing a well-known band called **'The Music Maestro Five'** to support the Choir. Rehearsals with the band should be underway within the next few weeks.